Nikky-Guninder Kaur Singh is the Crawford Family Professor and Chair of the department of Religious Studies at Colby College. She is the author of several books, which include *The Feminine Principle in the Sikh Vision of the Transcendent* (1993), *The Verses of the Sikh Gurus* (2001), *The Birth of the Khalsa* (2005), *Cosmic Symphony* (2008), and *Sikhism: An Introduction* (I.B.Tauris, 2011). She serves as the Co-Chair of the Sikh Studies Section of the American Academy of Religion.

"We need books like this one. It will introduce Punjabi literature to new audiences, providing a sense of the broad scope of Punjabi literature over time, and its achievements. We hear from Sufi poets – Baba Farid, as well as Bulhe Shah and Waris Shah – alongside the Sikh Gurus and other saints included in the Sikh sacred scripture. We hear modern voices, who embraced new styles and genres while adhering to the particular cadence and content of the Punjabi language. I hope this is a beginning, that it will inspire due attention to Punjabi literature, which has so little written about it in English, and so little available in translation. Our understanding of South Asian literature, and indeed world literature, demands this attention."

Anne Murphy
Chair in Punjabi Language Literature and Sikh Studies
University of British Columbia

"Nikky-Guninder Kaur Singh lucidly narrates five centuries of the literary and cultural history of Punjab through the voices of the region's most beloved poets. Her beautiful English renditions of the verses of eleven prominent Punjabi literary figures (ranging from the medieval Sufi poet Baba Farid and the much revered Sikh Guru Nanak to the contemporary feminist Amrita Pritam), and her insightful discussion of the significance of their poetry in the context of their times, provide refreshing frameworks through which to appreciate the complex interactions between disparate traditions in the region. Her analysis boldly challenges the rigid communalist boundaries that have been imposed on the Punjab's rich pluralistic heritage by contemporary discourses of nationalism in South Asia. Students of South Asian literatures, cultures, and religions will find this book to be a sensitively-written and accessible introduction to Punjabi literary culture in all of its diversity and complexity."

Ali Asani
Professor of Indo-Muslim and Islamic Religion and Cultures
Harvard University

"In these powerful and lyrical translations, Nikky Singh penetrates the surface of interreligious violence in the Punjab and reveals to us another world where Sikhs, Muslims, and Hindus share a rich treasure of vivid images of ordinary life and a brilliant vision of love, both carnal and divine. *Of Sacred and Secular Desire* brings into the mainstream of world poetry a great tradition that for far too long awaited an extraordinary translator like Nikky Singh to do it justice. The book is a most unusual combination of extraordinary beauty and great scholarly importance."

Wendy Doniger
Mircea Eliade Distinguished Service Professor of the History of Religions
University of Chicago

Of Sacred and Secular Desire

**An Anthology of
Lyrical Writings from the Punjab**

Nikky-Guninder Kaur Singh

I.B. TAURIS
LONDON · NEW YORK

Published in 2012 by I.B.Tauris & Co Ltd
6 Salem Road, London W2 4BU
175 Fifth Avenue, New York NY 10010
www.ibtauris.com

Distributed in the United States and Canada Exclusively by Palgrave Macmillan
175 Fifth Avenue, New York NY 10010

ISBN: 978 1 84885 883 1 (HB)
           978 1 84885 884 8 (PB)

A full CIP record for this book is available from the British Library
A full CIP record is available from the Library of Congress

Library of Congress Catalog Card Number: available

Printed and bound in Great Britain by TJ International Ltd, Padstow, Cornwall
from camera-ready copy edited and supplied by the author

FOR MY SARAH

CONTENTS

GLOSSARY

Ain	Arabic letter similar to the letter *Ghain*, distinguished only by a single superscript dot
Ajj	today
Alif	first letter of the alphabet; cipher for Allah
Amrit	nectar of immortality
Andaj	species born from egg
Arbi	a root used as vegetable
Arti	praise; Guru Nanak's poem is the daily evening prayer for the Sikhs
Ashraf	claim a superior status among the Muslims on the Indian sub-continent because of their lineage to the Prophet and foreign ancestry. The *Ajlaf* (non-Ashrafs) being local converts to Islam were regarded inferior
Azadi	freedom
Azrail	angel of death
Baba	designation for an elderly man
Bahadur	hero
Bahana	excuse
Bani	speech; voice; for the Sikhs poetry enshrined in the Guru Granth
Bansari	flute
Baqa	subsistence in God having annihilated the self/ego
Barat	wedding party from the groom's side
Bhagat/ bhakta	lover of God in the Indic tradition
Bhain	sister
Bhajan	devotional song
Bhakti	love for God
Bhangra	folk dance of the Punjab
Bhasha	language
Boli	speech, language

Brahma	creator god
Burki	a tiny bite of food
Burqa	women's clothing which covers the entire body, including the face with a grille over the eyes
Buta	pattern of buds on fabric including shawls and carpets
Chakki	hand-operated millstone
Chakor	partridge; lover of the moon in myth and poetry
Charkha	spinning wheel
Chela	disciple
Chenab	one of the five rivers of the Punjab, famous for the love legends of Heer-Ranjha, Sohni-Mahiwal, Mirza-Sahiban, and Sassi-Punnu
Chetar	(March–April) first month of the Indian calendar
Chillah	forty days' seclusion, common among Sufis
Churi	handmade bread crumbled with butter and molasses
Crore	10 million
Darbar	imperial audience
Dargah	shrine built on the grave of a Sufi saint
Darshan	seeing (usually a deity or revered figure)
Devi	goddess
Devnagari	Sanskrit script, basis for north Indian scripts including Gurmukhi
Devta	god
Dharamraj	god of judgment
Dharti	earth
Dhikr	remembering, especially the repetition of the names of God and mystical utterances
Dhur	from the very origins
Dhur ki bani	revealed word
Divali	Indian festival of Lights celebrated in the autumn
Doha	usually edifactory couplet with two rhyming verses. Each verse consists of 24 syllables following a prescribed pattern
Fana	annihilation of the individual ego
Farman	imperial order
Fatwa	legal judgment
Geet	song
Ghain	Arabic letter like *ain*, but with a dot
Ghazal	lyric love poem in mono-rhyme usually not longer than 14 verses
Giddha	folk dance for women with poetic refrains

Gokula-Mathura	village of Mathura on the River Yamuna where Lord Krishna was born and raised. The region resonates with the enchantment of his flute
Gulzar	rose-garden style of Arabic writing in letters filled with flowers and other motifs
Gurdwara	Sikh space for worship
Gurmukhi	script developed by the Sikh Gurus and later standardized as the script of modern Punjabi in India
Guru	teacher
Gutka	small book of sacred poetry carried by Sikh men and women
Hadith	"saying tradition", regarding the words and sayings of the Prophet Muhammad transmitted orally
Hafiz	"preserver", someone who knows the holy Qur'an by heart
Hamad/hamd	praise; an invocation to God, Prophet Muhammad and Sufi saints, which was also a literary convention of the *qissa* narratives
Haqiqat	truth, reality
Harmal	plant burnt to ward off the evil eye in West Asian folk practices. Used by Pre-Islamic Zoroastrians in Iran
Harmandar	sacred and secular center of the Sikhs in Amritsar. It was originally constructed by Guru Arjan to enshrine the Sikh sacred text compiled in 1604. Later embellished by Maharaja Ranjit Singh, it is the modern Golden Temple
Hazrat	honorific preceding the name of Masters and Prophets
Hing	asophetia; used as a spice in cooking
Holi	Indian spring festival of colors during which people spray colored water and powder on each other
Iccha	desire
Ilm	knowledge
Indra	god of storm
Ishq	love
Izzat	honor
Jali	carved latticework in front of windows or balconies
Japuji	the first hymn in the Guru Granth, recited in the morning by devout Sikhs
Jatti	female belonging to the agricultural class, connotes a sturdy woman
Jeraj	species born from the womb

Ka'ba	the most sacred site in Islam. Muslims around the world offer their five daily prayers turned in the direction of the Ka'ba located in Mecca, Saudi Arabia
Kabit	quatrain
Kafi	genre of devotional poetry meant to be sung. Often accompanied by instruments. It is said to have the Arabic mono-rhyme *qasida* as its precursor. The central verse is repeated to bring out the force of the mystical lyric
Kalma	Islamic prayer
Kaleje da tukra	"sweetheart", "beloved"
Kanya	premenstrual virgin
Kauda	a carnivorous demon in Sikh hagiography
Kavi	poet
Kavita	poem
Kesha	long hair (one of the five symbols of the Sikhs)
Khalifa	caliph, head of Islamic (Sunni) community
Khes	cotton blanket
Khichri	dish of rice and lentils, also means to mix things up
Khuda	God
Khurak	dietary intake
Kikkali Kali	a girl's rhyme
Kikkar	acacia tree
Kirpa	benevolence
Kirtan	singing of sacred verse
Koel	cuckoo-bird; symbol of longing
Kos	measurement of length, equivalent of approximately two miles
Kotwal	magistrate
Kumari	virgin, daughter
Lal	ruby, red, denotes lover as well
Lakh	one hundred thousand
Lala	form of address for a Hindu businessman
Langar	meals in Sufi shrines, Sikh Gurdwaras and Hindu Mandirs
Lassi	yoghurt drink diluted with water
Laxmi	goddess of wealth
Laylat ul-qadr	"night of power", the night of the fist revelation of the Qur'an on approximately 27 Ramadan
Leek laganee	"put a line", to blemish or bring dishonor
Lori	lullaby
Mahakaviraj	poet laureate

Mali	gardener
Malik ash-shu'ara	"king of poets"
Mandir	Hindu space of worship
Masjid	Muslim space of worship
Mast	intoxicated
Maulud	poem celebrating the Prophet Muhammad's birthday
Maulvi	title for Muslim religious scholars
Mazhab	religion
Mian	form of address for a male Muslim
Minbar	pulpit in the mosque where the prayer leader stands to deliver his sermon
Mira/Meera	medieval Hindu princess passionately in love with Lord Krishna; her popular songs make her the most prominent female saint of India
Mufti	Muslim scholar with the power to issue *fatwas* (legal judgments)
Muhabbat	love
Mukti	Hindu ideal: freedom from the cycle of birth and death
Mullah	Muslim male educated in Islamic theology and sacred law
Murid	disciple
Murshid	Master (*murshid* and *murid* pair in Sufism parallel the *Guru* and *chela* in Bhakti)
Mutth	palmful (pl. *mutthan*)
Nadar	benevolent gaze
Naksh	cursive handwriting
Namaz	Muslim prayer
Narak	hell
Nasheele	intoxicated
Nasta'liq	"hanging" form of writing evolved in Persia which spread to Turkey and India
Nauratan	nine (*nau*) jewels (*ratan*)
Nishan	sign, stamp, banner
Nuqta	diacritical point
Nur	light
Pandits	Hindu religious scholars and officials who conduct rituals and rites of passage
Pir	saints; "fairy godmothers" of the Punjab
Puja	Hindu mode of worship
Punjab	five (*punj*) + waters (*ab*); the land of the five rivers of Sutlej, Beas, Ravi, Jhelum, and Chenab
Pyar	love

Qasida	a long poem, normally an ode, with single rhyme
Qateb	in the Guru Granth refers to the Semitic texts: the Torah, the Zabur, the Injil, and the Qur'an
Qaumi	national
Qayyam	eternally existing, immutable
Qazi/Qadi	Muslim judge ruling in accordance with the Sharia
Qissa	Punjabi literary genre based in Arabic and Persian narrative traditions but utilizing India meters. Starting in the seventeenth century, the narratives became very popular as both high literature and popular entertainment
Qurbat	nearness
Qutb	pole, axis
Rabab	Arab fiddle; bowed instrument with two or three stings
Rabb	God
Rahmat	compassion
Rasa	"juice", aesthetic flavor
Rasana	"tongue", sense or faculty of taste
Rashtra	nation
Ruba'i	quatrain with the rhyming pattern aaba; also epigram
Rumala	cloth for wrapping gifts; covering for the Sikh sacred text
Safina	"boat", portable anthology of Persian verse
Sain	husband, lover
Sajda	prostration
Sajjan thag	"sajan" which means good, ironically, is the name of a robber (*thag*) in Sikh hagiography
Saki	cupbearer
Sanyasi	ascetic
Sarasvati	goddess of knowledge
Sardar	form of address for a male Sikh
Saropa	from head to foot; robe of honor
Sassi	romantic heroine
Sayyid	descendants of Prophet Muhammad through his daughter Fatima and son-in-law Ali
Sehra	a veil of flowers or pearls worn by bridegroom
Setaj	species born from bodily secretions
Shair	poet
Shakti	female power
Sharbat	nectar, cool drink in the summer heat
Sharia	sacred law of Islam

Shish mahal	"glass palace", a room with walls decorated with mirrors
Shivratri	night of the new moon and Hindu festival in honor of Lord Shiva
Siharfi	"thirty-letter poem"; "golden alphabet" or alphabetic odes composed by folk poets
Sitar	a stringed instrument with a long hollow neck and a gourd resonating chamber, it is predominant in Hindustani classical music
Sloka	couplet with 16 syllables in each line (sometimes printed as quatrains with 8 syllables in each line)
Suad	taste
Suhag	wedding songs
Swarag/ suarag	heaven
Tariqa	path for Sufis; the fraternity or order in the mystical way
Tasbih	prayer beads
Tawhid	declaration of the oneness of god
Tulsi	'basil', herb used in Hindu rituals for its sacred power. Tulsi is also the famous medieval Indian poet who composed the epic *Ramcharitmanas* devoted to the Hindu God Rama
Twarikh	date
Urs'	"wedding", death anniversary of a saint commemorated as one whose soul has been wedded to God
Utbhuj	species born from the earth
Veda	ancient Hindu texts in Sanskrit language (oral texts produced between 1500 BCE and 500 BCE)
Vishnu	preserver god; he descends in many forms including that of Lord Krishna and Lord Rama
Wahdat al-wujud	oneness of being
Zamin	"ground", a form of poem, which is imitated exactly
Zanana	the women's quarters of the palace
Zaban	"tongue", language

PREFACE

Punjab, the gateway to the Indian Subcontinent, welcomed people from diverse regions, religions, and ethnicities, and as they settled on its fertile soil, they developed a common language called Punjabi. In contrast to this popular language, the court language was Persian from the time of Mahmud of Ghazna (997–1030) to the fall of the Sikh Kingdom (1849), and the "sacred" languages for the majority of the inhabitants were Sanskrit, Arabic, and Gurmukhi. But for centuries ordinary Muslims, Sikhs, and Hindus in north India shared their everyday feelings, experiences, and understanding of the world in the Punjabi language. Unfortunately, after the conquest of the Punjab, this linguistic world was ruptured. Punjabi became exclusively linked with the Sikhs, Urdu with the Muslims, and Hindi with the Hindus. Their sense of togetherness was painfully ripped asunder. This anthology brings them together again. It collects the lyrics that the Punjabi people heard, sang, recited, performed, and read together. In this way we can retrieve "the profound dimension from which tradition comes down to those now living" (Gadamer, *Truth and Method*, pp. 463–4).

There is a visceral reason for translating these lyrics into English too: the poetry in my mother tongue transports me from my New England mode of being down the waters of memory to my home and my parents in the Punjab, and puts me in touch with my deepest roots. My childhood home was the Punjabi University at Patiala, set up in postcolonial Punjab for the advancement of Punjabi language, literature, and culture (the "Hebrew" University in Israel perhaps is the only other University founded on "language"). The linguistic divisions fomented under the British Raj had led to the tragic Partition of the Subcontinent. The founders of the Punjabi University knew well that human language does not simply mirror reality; it has the power to transform reality, and so language was to be the resource for understanding both the heritage of the Punjab as well as its entrance into a dynamic new future. My family literally lived on the upper floor of the University located in the lush Baradari Gardens. My father was an eminent scholar, and our home bustled with poets and writers who have been inspirational for me over the years. I absorbed the elemental Punjabi of Bullhe Shah and Amrita Pritam with Punjab's dry summer heat and its drenching monsoon. By hearing them now in the midst of sparkling snows of Maine I retrieve my lost past. Translation forces me to read the original works closely, and thereby connects me with the poets at their artistic heights. As I begin to hear the words again – those that I have been taking for granted and have been accustomed to for years – suddenly become uncertain, full of mystery. The process of translation has certainly been an "adventure," which says Gadamer, "interrupts the customary course of events, but is positively and significantly related to the context which it interrupts." And yes, I have emerged from this venturing out into the unexpected both "enriched and more mature" (*T&M*, p. 69).

My love for Punjabi was deepened when I came to the USA to finish high school in Virginia where I began to long for the words that I had heard from the lips of my mother and grandmother. In the Punjab I attended Victorian schools, and English had been my favorite subject. But when I read "Passage to India" by Walt Whitman in the USA, I realized the false consciousness I had absorbed growing up in postcolonial India. So I made a special effort each summer when I went home to study medieval Punjabi texts with scholars at the Punjabi University. As an undergraduate at Wellesley College, I wrote my honors thesis on sacred Punjabi poetry. In America I also developed a real fondness for English where I experienced it as a living language rather than a dead language written by poets long past like Shakespeare. They say that the language one dreams in is one's mother tongue – but I dream in both Punjabi and English (depends on the scene!), and love them equally. My goal in my translations is to reproduce their essential parity. The genuine affinity between languages that I experienced going back and forth Punjabi and English confirms Gadamer's view that the "translation process fundamentally contains the whole secret of how human beings come to an understanding of the world and communicate with each other" (*T&M*, p. 548).

It is impossible to fully thank everybody involved in this project, so just a few words. My thanks to my students at Colby for inspiring me to explore the confluence of those deeply personal and academic dimensions of my heritage. To my editor Mr. Alex Wright for welcoming this project that has meant so much to me in so many ways. To my colleague and neighbor Elizabeth Sagaser for reading my manuscript under extreme time pressure, and giving me her valuable suggestions. To our Religious Studies majors Lizzie Poteet and Spencer Kasko for helping me out with their cheer and technical expertise. To Cecile Rault for her design and production of this volume. To Kate Baxter and the Inverness community for their enthusiastic reception of my work. To Bhabiji Harjeet for getting me out when I would enter a maze. To Amarjit Chandan and Gurcharan Rampuri for sending me signed copies of their enriching poetry. To Inni Kaur, Geetanjali Chanda, Laurel York, Mary-Ellen Fitzpatrick, Kara Gorczyca, and Jim and Mary Crawford for their warm friendship. To Mom O'Neil for her encouraging phonecalls from Montana. To Bira who brings my past back to life for me. And to Harry and Sarah for letting me live my dreams. A special thanks goes to the Punjabi University at Patiala: it was a great honor for me to receive a fellowship and be invited to give a lecture last December; but to be greeted as the "daughter of the University" made it a golden moment. These words charge me to take up my "daughterly" duty, and they reveal the phenomenal force of language.

INTRODUCTION

Though divided today between India and Pakistan, the Punjab originally extended all the way from the Afghani capital of Kabul to the Indian capital of Delhi. Since the Hindu Kush Mountains of Afghanistan formed its northern frontier, different religions and ideas crossed through the Khyber Pass and made their way into the Punjab. It was here that the West Asian tradition of Islam encountered South Asian civilization. Trade was carried on abundantly and battles were fought vehemently, but exquisite lyrics from the subterranean depths of the human psyche were produced here too. In this volume I wish to bring some samples of these lyrics to an English-speaking readership.

Poetry has been an essential part of the living experience of the people in the Indo Pakistan Subcontinent. Tiny steatite seals from pre-historic civilization reveal the imaginative worldview of the earliest inhabitants settled on the banks of the Indus (2500–1900 BCE). In one of the images we see human figures, a rhino, lion, buffalo, and an elephant surrounding a central figure seated in a yogic posture. There is something written above, but since we cannot decipher the script we can only wonder about the intimacy the people had with the bounty and vitality of nature. Later, the Indo-Aryans who came from Central Asia with their horses in search of land and lucre settled in the fertile region, which is now the modern Punjab. While grazing their cattle and growing their crops, they created the vast Vedic corpus in sophisticated Sanskrit, leaving us with some of the earliest and most beautiful poems in our human history.

The land of the five waters (*punj+ab* in Persian) – rivers Sutlej, Ravi, Beas, Jhelum, and Chenab – has constantly stirred the psyche of its people. In 326 BCE Alexander the Great conquered the Punjab, and he and his successors left some Greek cultural and linguistic influences on the region. Over the centuries, the lure of the land of the five rivers brought in waves of other foreigners as well – Scythians, Sassanids, Huns, Afghans, Persians, Turks, Mughals, and closer to our own times, the British. Of course many ferocious battles were fought. But as different ethnic, cultural, religious, and political groups came together, the intrinsic spirit of Punjab's soil was colored with vibrant new patterns, new worldviews, and new languages. Punjabi poetry is a dynamic flow coming from these encounters.

The origins of the Punjabi language still remain rather ambiguous. It starts in the early part of the second millennium. By then Arabic and Persian were making their entry into the world dominated by Sanskrit with its Devnagari script. But the elite languages did not seep into the daily parlance of the masses. Common folks spoke vernacular dialects that varied from region to region, and used local scripts for their daily accounts. Basically Indo-Aryan, but including Arabic and Persian vocabulary, the 13th century Indo-Persian poet Amir Khusrau identified a distinct dialect in the Lahore region which he called "Lahauri." This dialect later developed into Punjabi, a language that is written in three different scripts: Sikhs use the Gurmukhi script developed by their Gurus, the Punjabi Muslims of Pakistan and India use the Indo-Persian script, and Hindus (and some Sikhs) use the Devnagari script.

The scripture of the Sikhs, the Guru Granth, marks a major event for Punjabi literature. Compiled by the fifth Sikh Guru in 1604, the 1430-paged volume is written entirely in the Gurmukhi script. The text was compiled during Emperor Akbar's reign when the Mughal Empire was at its zenith. The leading Indo-Muslim scholar Annemarie Schimmel notes, "In 1598 Akbar visited the prolific Guru Arjan, who compiled the holy book of the Sikhs."[1] The pluralist vision of the Mughal emperor not only brought people together for inter-religious discussions and produced a new "Divine Faith" (*Din-i-Ilahi*), but also gave impetus to the rise of vernacular languages and their literature. Interestingly, just when Persian was becoming the lingua franca of the Mughal administration, the regional language of Punjabi on the north-western periphery of the Indian peninsula was being crystallized by the Sikh Gurus. The Gurmukhi script for Punjabi evolved from the *lande/mahajani* business shorthand used by the first Sikh Guru (1469–1539) during his apprenticeship in granaries and storehouses. The Fifth Guru (Arjan, 1563–1606) gathered the songs of his predecessor Sikh Gurus and those of Sufi and Hindu saints into the Guru Granth. As far back as 1781, the English scholar Charles Wilkins described the language of the Guru Granth as "a mixture of *Persian, Arabic* and some *Sanscrit*, grafted upon the provincial dialect of Punjab, which is a kind of Hindoovee, or, as it is vulgarly called by us, *moors*."[2] This text, the Guru Granth, is the first anthology of Punjabi poetry.

It is here that we find four hymns and 130 couplets composed by the first recognized Punjabi poet Sheikh Farid (1175–1265). Though some scholars question the identity of the author,[3] most believe he is indeed the venerated Sheikh Farid, one of the founding fathers of the popular Chishti Sufi order in India. As such, the compositions form the earliest extant example of Punjabi writing. Sheikh Farid was a devout Muslim who settled in Pakpattan on the river Sutlej in central Punjab. Islam had come to the Sindh as early as 711, but it was not till Mahmud of Ghazna started his conquests around 1000 that the Punjab developed several Muslim religious centers and a substantial Muslim population. By the late eleventh century, Delhi became the capital of Muslim dynasties, and the Punjab being the caravan route from the Middle and Near East to Delhi, was enriched with Sufi shrines, *khanqas* (hospices), *langars* (food halls), and mosques. Fleeing the Mongol invasions of the twelfth century, Sheikh Farid's ancestors left their home in central Asia and came to the Punjab. He was born near Multan and was named after the Persian Sufi poet and philosopher, Farid-ud-din Attar.

Although Sheikh Farid's ideas were derived from the Sufi models of Iran, Iraq, and Central Asia, he expressed them in the local language and metaphors, and became enormously successful in promoting Islam amongst many ethnically distinct groups on the Indian Subcontinent. In hopes of receiving his *baraka* (spiritual power) and favors like good crops, female fertility, cure from disease, millions of villagers have visited his tomb and shrine at Pakpattan. With Sheikh Farid the Chishti movement gained tremendous influence, surpassing the Qadiri, Suhrawardi, and the Naqshbandi Sufi orders. Guru Nanak, the founder of the Sikh religion, was born several centuries after Farid, and he too was attracted by the Chishti saint's message. Sikh historians recount that during his travels Guru Nanak met with Sheikh Farid's twelfth successor from whom he procured the compositions. When the Fifth Guru created the holy volume for the evolving Sikh community, he enshrined those compositions.[4] Along with Sheikh Farid, the Guru Granth contains the verses of Guru Nanak's Muslim companion Mardana, the Sufi Sheikh Bhikan, the Muslim bards Satta and Balvand and several Hindu saints like Namdev, Ravidas, Jaidev, Beni, Trilochan, Parmananda, Sadhana, Ramananda, Dhanna, Pipa, Sain, Sur Das, Sundar, and the Bhatts.[5] Almost three hundred hymns of the popular North Indian saint Kabir are also included. The Sikh sacred book extends over several centuries and various geographical regions, and brings together a plurality of religions, cultures, ethnicities, and languages. Unfortunately, its pluralism lies smothered in the contemporary global reality. In 1947 the British drew up the Radcliffe Line dividing the Indian Subcontinent along religious lines. Carved out of India, Pakistan was the first modern nation founded on the basis of religious identity. The province of Punjab (as was Bengal) was split between the two nations. A horrific holocaust ensued as millions of Muslims, Hindus, and Sikhs began to migrate across the national border, and to this day, that ghastly past continues to haunt the South Asian psyche and its politics. The process of fragmentation began once the British took over the Punjab after the Anglo-Sikh wars in 1849. Unlike our sharp modern day divisions, the religious boundaries amongst the Punjabis had been fluid. Most spoke local Punjabi dialects, and were cross-ethnically bound together. Anxious about their strength and solidarity, the new rulers incited divisions of religion, language, ethnicity, and nation. In the Punjabi speaking province, "Urdu" was made the official language. Land-holding Muslims in the northern United Provinces were prompted to establish the Muslim league in 1906 to represent Muslim interests. In 1909 separate electorates were instituted for the Indian population. In *Violent Belongings* Kavita Daiya exposes the British Raj's success in producing Hindus and Muslims "as inimical, politically opposed, and homogeneous communities that belonged in two different nations," which led to one of the most bloody events in the history of modern nation-formation.[6]

More than half a century later, people who once enjoyed a symbiotic relationship, are embroiled in conflict. Fires of sectarianism and hatred continue to burn. It was humiliating for me as a Punjabi to hear that the sole surviving perpetrator of the Mumbai terrorist attacks is a Punjabi speaker! What a contrast to the Punjabi revolutionary Udham Singh (1899–1940) who called himself "Ram Mohammad Singh Azad" – embodying the religious unity of the Punjabis (Hindu "Ram", Muslim "Mohammad", and Sikh "Singh") in their struggle for freedom (*azadi*).[7] A region with mutuality and openness amongst the major religions of the Punjab now breeds insularity and fanaticism. Historian Farina Mir criticizes the domination of South Asia and South Asian historiography "by the specter of the Partition": the shared experience of the Punjabis is obstructed by postcolonial political tensions between India and Pakistan, by the rhetoric accompanying the communal pogroms in India and

Pakistan, and by the "Partition industry" – the flurry of recent scholarship, which tries to understand the violence perpetrated in 1947.[8] With her focus on the tradition of Heer-Ranjha narratives, Mir provides an important antithesis to the narrowly communalist interpretation of Punjabi linguistic practices, publishing, and performance in nineteenth century Punjab. A few years earler Ali Asani, the expert in Indo-Muslim literature, wrote on the marginalization of the Sufi folk tradition by scholars of Indian Islam and its disdain by the *ashraf*, the religious and intellectual elite of the Muslim community.[9] Asani offers some fascinating equations made by the medieval Shiites in the Sindh and Gujarat rural areas: the Prophet with the Hindu deity Brahma, the Prophet's daughter Fatima with the Hindu goddess of knowledge Sarasvati, the first Shiite Imam Ali with the tenth avatar of the preserver deity Vishnu.[10] Such imaginings would be anathema for the intellectuals who have only been underscoring the elitist facets that demarcate and distinguish. We have been missing out on the all-embracing sentiments and experiences of the people. I have always felt that we need to shift our focus and hear their symphonic voice. This anthology brings together a wide range of Punjabi lyrics across religions, centuries, and nations as a reminder of the shared consciousness that is obscured by divisive politics and is in danger of being lost. This shared memory must have a future, as Katherine Stimpson says,[11] so that these recorded melodies will have the potential to transform the flames of conflict into flames of mutual respect and understanding.

Outline
The book begins with the medieval poets from the Guru Granth, the quintessential Punjabi text. From its vast repertoire I chose the Sikh Gurus Nanak (first author in the text) and Guru Arjan (its compiler and editor), the Chishti Master Sheikh Farid, and the Hindu saints Bhagat Namdev (1270–1350, low-caste calico-printer) and Bhagat Ravidas (1450–1520, low-caste tanner). These five represent the religious, aesthetic, and social variety informing the Sikh sacred volume. The Sikh Gurus desire the divine One, and feel it joyously as father and mother; as groom and as bride; as friend, brother, and sister. The Muslim Farid desires Allah, and prescribes ritual prayer and asceticism as the path to union. Bhagats Namdev and Ravidas desire the Divine, and palpably see it in the form of Hindu deities such as Krishna and Ram. *Bhakti* (devotion) was introduced as a parallel path to knowledge (*Jnana*) and action (*Karma*) in the Bhagavad Gita, which made the Supreme Being accessible to all devotees including women and men of the lowest Shudra class (Bhagavad Gita, 9: 22–23).

The devout from different Hindu classes began to approach the Divine in a loving relationship – as child, friend, servant or lover. The Bhakti movement took on force in the sixth century in the South and spread all over India, including the Punjab. As we read the poetry of Sufis and Bhagats enshrined in the Sikh sacred text, theoretical and doctrinal oppositions dissolve; together, the poems disclose "Islam", "Hinduism", "Sikhism" as artificial categories. The desires of the Guru Granth poets challenge scholars and theologians to reconsider their neat divisions and systematizations that have been constructed too simplistically and held up all too dogmatically. As the verses of "Sikh" Guru Nanak, "Muslim" Sheikh Farid, and "Hindu" Bhagat Namdev are read together, we begin to recognize the different features of our shared humanity, and overcome fear and alienation of the *other*. Images and symbols from different religious and cultural backgrounds represent our human capacity for peace and love.

This essential spirit of the Sikh sacred text forms the leitmotif for this entire volume. In Chapter 2 we enter the classical period of Punjabi poetry. Here we encounter the Sufi poets Bullhe Shah (1680–1758) – surnamed the "Rumi of Punjab,"[12] and Waris Shah (*ca.* 1722–1798). They are a part of the rich tradition of Punjabi Sufi poets including Sheikh Farid, Shah Husain (1538–1599), Sultan Bahu (1628–1691), Shah Sharaf (1659–1725), Ali Haidar (1690–1785), Farad Faqir (1720–90), Hashim Shah (1735–1843), Fazal Shah (1827–90), Mian Muhammad Baksh (1830–1907), and Ghulam Farid (1845–1905). These are the traditional dates for these poets but they are uncertain. About 30 years apart, Bullhe Shah and Waris Shah lived in an eighteenth-century Punjab that was fraught with internal battles and external invasions by the Persian Nadir Shah and the Afghani Ahmad Shah Durrani. The religious persecution by the Emperor Aurangzeb (1618–1707) had demoralized the people. The Mughal Empire founded by Babur in 1526 was shrinking; the commercial East India Company was expanding its military dominance. The Punjab became a battleground for the Persians, Afghanis, the British, and the Sikhs – each group fighting to establish its own empire.

Against such a violent external backdrop, our Sufi poets found peace in the inner world of love. They desire the Divine most romantically, most tenderly. Exalting *ishq* or *muhabbat* (love) their supreme religious principle, Bullhe Shah and Waris Shah brilliantly fuse erotic and sublime elements.[13] Their paradigmatic figures are Heer and Ranjha, the lovers (*ashiq*), who lose themselves utterly in their love for the beloved. Indeed these Muslim poets seem to profess their faith as *la ilaha illa'l-'ishq* ("There is no God but Love") – they poetically identify Allah with Love in this new version of the first pillar of Islam.[14] Belonging to its open and mystical dimension, Bullhe Shah and Waris Shah approach Islam in a personal and experiential way. Like the verse of Sheikh Farid, their poetry is sustained by their love for Allah, the Prophet Muhammad, and Sufi Masters. And like Sheikh Farid, they opted for the indigenous Punjabi over the Arabic of the holy Qur'an or the sophisticated Persian of the literati, and thus they became instantly popular with the masses. Waris Shah draws upon his rich literary Punjabi heritage, and even honors Sheikh Farid at the outset of *Heer* (the text named after his immortal heroine). In unmatched beauty he reproduces the legendary romance between Heer and Ranjha – the Juliet and Romeo of the Punjab. The Indian Sufi poets transformed the predominantly male metaphor of Persian and Arabic Sufi poetry into a female seeking union with her divine Beloved, which was the pattern of indigenous Bhakti poets.

Though today Punjabi is primarily identified with the Sikhs, the Muslims spoke and wrote extensively in Punjabi, and the Sikhs made use of Braj and Persian, the chief north Indian literary languages of the later Mughal period. After Guru Arjan had compiled the Guru Granth, Braj became popular amongst Sikh writers, but they used the Gurmukhi script. The revered Sikh theologian Bhai Gurdas (1551–1636, the scribe for the Guru Granth) composed ballads in Punjabi and couplets in Braj. The Book of the Tenth Guru, known as the Dasam Granth, is composed almost entirely in Braj.[15] Persian continued to be the official language during the rule of Maharaja Ranjit Singh (1798–1839) but a patron of Punjabi literature, he had several Sanskrit and Persian works translated into Punjabi. During Sikh rule Muslim poets like Hashim Shah (1735–1843), Ahmad Yar (1768–1848), and Qadir Yar (1802–92) produced highly sophisticated works in the Punjabi language. Starting with Sheikh Farid, Muslim poets have contributed vitally to the development of Punjabi as a literary language. The sonorous rhythms of communal harmony created by Bullhe Shah and Waris Shah have been hugely popular over the centuries. On the global scene today, Indian and Pakistani singers are synthesizing their lyrics with reggae and hip-hop both at home and in diasporic communities. Indeed, the poets who sang of love as the utmost divine quality of the human race have become the beloved poets of the Punjab. The Muslims, Sikhs, and Hindus have proudly embraced Bullhe Shah and Waris Shah as their own.

Chapter 3 is devoted to Bhai Vir Singh (1872–1957), Dhani Ram Chatrik (1876–1954), and Firoz Din Sharaf (1898–1955), the renowned "makers of modern Punjabi literature." They were born into Sikh, Hindu, and Muslim families respectively in the Punjab, after the British annexed it in 1849. Since it was the last of the Indian provinces to succumb to British rule, it was also the last to be exposed to Western ideas and Western education. But when it experienced modern influence, the Punjab was quick to respond and interact. Christian missions, English schools and colleges with their innovative curriculums, brought the Punjab into the orbit of a new consciousness. The Presbyterian mission set up a printing press, which produced translations into Punjabi from the Bible and from English literature. The first book to be printed in the Gurmukhi script was the Bible itself. Ironically, the introduction to Western ideologies under the British Raj fostered the development of indigenous cultural traditions and the vernacular Punjabi literature. Poets like Bhai Vir Singh, Chatrik, and Sharaf responded dynamically to the challenges of their rapid social and cultural changes. Each recognized the essential bond between culture and language, and seizing the new energy around them, they transformed Punjabi language into a powerful medium to express new literary, artistic, and social ideas.

And they produced volumes. Bhai Vir Singh, for instance, published eight collections of poetry, four novels, a play, five biographies, and nine major texts that he meticulously annotated and commented upon – while keeping up with his journalism. He was the leading figure in the Singh Sabha, the dynamic Sikh renaissance movement, which aspired to revive Punjabi culture on the principles of the Sikh Gurus. Dhani Ram Chatrik was born into a Hindu family. He was also a prolific writer, but he was more concerned with the political, social, and economic issues of his times. In his breathtakingly poignant verse, Chatrik addresses the problems of colonialism, nepotism, unemployment, and exploitation. Along with his creative works, Chatrik standardized the type set for the Gurmukhi script, and published major Punjabi reference works like the Punjabi encyclopedia and the Punjabi dictionary – the first of their kind. Firoz Din Sharaf was a dedicated Muslim, and in spite of the anti-Punjabi sentiment prevailing in some circles, he adopted his mother tongue Punjabi for literary expression. Sharaf's intellectual kinsmen including Mohammad Iqbal, Ahmad Nadeem Qasmi, Faiz Ahmad Faiz, Sa'adat Hasan Manto, composed in Urdu. When Dr. P. L. Chatterjee (the Vice Chancellor of the Punjab University, who originally belonged to Bengal) suggested that Punjabi replace Urdu since it was the real vernacular language of the Punjab, waves of vehement anger spread across the province.[16] Undeterred by communal hostilities, Sharaf dedicated his life to the advancement of Punjabi language. He enriched Punjabi verse by bringing in Persian and Arabic vocabulary and metaphors from his Muslim heritage. Sharaf was an enormously popular figure at poetry symposiums, and became the recipient of many awards. By his mid-thirties he had produced seven volumes of poetry. With such literary giants, Punjabi language and sensibility acquired exciting new themes and genres. Our three poets belong to a linguistic and cultural world shared by the Hindus, Muslims and Sikhs alike. But as their religious communities increasingly came into conflict during the later years of the British Raj, linguistic parochialism dismembered their common mother tongue.

This work concludes with Amrita Pritam (1919–2005), the most celebrated poet of postcolonial India. Born in Gujranwala in pre-partitioned Punjab, Amrita closely witnessed its traumatic division. In her "Ode to Waris Shah," she urges the Sufi poet to grapple with the unimaginable gendered and sexual violence that was being afflicted on the hundreds and thousands of Punjabi women at that time. The poet who triumphed splendidly in conveying the tragedy of his one heroine, how could he be lying silently in his grave? Pritam's elegiac intertextual poem brought her instant fame. Upon her migration to India, she worked for the All India Radio until 1961, after which she devoted herself entirely to writing. Though Punjabi was her main medium of expression, Pritam also wrote extensively in Hindi and Urdu. Soon she came to be known on either side of the Indo-Pak Border as the "voice of the Punjab." Amrita Pritam has authored numerous novels, collections of short stories, and volumes of poetry. Her novel *Pinjar* was translated by the eminent historian Khushwant Singh, and was later adapted into film by director Chandra Prakash Dwivedi. She is the first woman recipient of the prestigious Sahitya Academy Award, and the first woman to receive the Padma Shri as well. She was awarded the Jnanpith for her lifetime contributions to Punjabi literature in 1982. Most of the poems that I translated here come from her award winning collections. With her deep feminist empathy Amrita Pritam discloses multiple scenarios in which Indian women are horribly objectified and victimized. The poet courageously questions modern assumptions about identity and culture. Her subtle critique of seemingly lovely rituals and customs strikingly pinpoints the atrocious sexism festering Indian society. Her death on October 31, 2005 is a great loss for the South Asian literary world.

From Sheikh Farid to Amrita Pritam, these eleven poets present the full spectrum of Punjabi poetry, and together offer a wonderful reservoir of powerful and delightful verse – highly metaphysical, startlingly physical. Along with psychic angst and spiritual longing and cosmic celebrations, these poets express political rage, economic deprivation, societal hegemonies, and gender bias. Literary styles from both West Asia and South Asia find their confluence here: the *ghazal, qissa, rubai, kafi* from Persian and Arabic, sonorously join with the *doha, kabit, and sloka* from Sanskrit. Similarly, images from West Asia and South Asia are magically spliced. In the poetry of Waris Shah, for example, we find Ranjha, the Punjabi Romeo, in a pastoral setting playing the flute – a primordial Krishna figure from the Hindu tradition. But when driven away from his beloved, the imagery comes from the Islamic tradition: he is compared with Adam expelled from the Garden of Eden, his bewilderment rendered analogous to Noah caught in the Flood. Rather than irreconcilable differences, we recover equality and convergence between the Islamic and Hindu religions. Throughout Punjabi poetry, the recurrent pattern of intensity and ultimacy of life is interlaced with daily chores and agrarian fluctuations.

Overall, bringing about the meeting of "sacred" and "secular" poetry is a meaningful process. In our dualized intellectual frameworks, religion and art are usually in conflict, thought and desire are two opposite processes, the divine and the human are two separate spheres. Religious and secular poetry is rarely published in the same anthology. These Punjabi poets express *desires*, physical and metaphysical, that shatter such polarizations. Whether it is the "desire" for the transcendent Divine or the "desire" to be treated humanely, our poets think with their senses, they perceive the Divine in the sensuousness of everyday experience, they remind us of our human responsibilities. Their poetic arabesques open a new horizon for us to reflect on the political, the social, and the moral in our postmodern world.

Approach

Translating of course is a difficult task, and we are all familiar with Robert Frost's dictum, "poetry is what is lost in translation." A translation cannot ever replace the original. With his phenomenological analysis of the lyric, Gadamer makes my task even more daunting: "It is in the lyric that language appears in its pure essence, so that all the possibilities of language, and even of the concept, are as it were germinally contained within it."[17] When sound and meaning are interwoven "to the point of being indivisible," what does a translator do? How does a translator convey the dynamic alliteration, assonance, rhyme, and overall aesthetic efficacy of the original melodies of these great Punjabi poets? Now how does a translator transmit the taste from one tongue to another?

Somehow I don't think scholarly exercises and contrived rhyming schemes work. A translator must feel the poetic and musical quality of the original. Actually, Gadamer's advice comes in very handy: "you must sharpen your ear, you must realize that when you take a word in your mouth, you have not taken up some arbitrary tool which can be thrown in a corner if it doesn't do the job, but you are committed to a line of thought that comes from afar and reaches on beyond you."[18] The original lyrics must be heard in the language of the poets, every bit must be respected, and the lyrics must make their entry into the mouth of the translator and move about freely so their creative power will rebound fluently with its own sound and sense. The problem Gadamer diagnoses is with our misunderstanding of language: when we view it merely as a stock of words and phrases, then, like computers and parrots, we simply plug in conventional equations and keep ourselves buried under the load of linguistic pre-schematizations. But when we realize "language is the single word, whose virtuality opens for us the infinity of discourse" we enter new horizons.[19] A translator from Punjabi into English must give up old habits and venture out to discover new expressions. As translators we must allow ourselves to be possessed by the original Punjabi verses and rhythms that come from far away; inspired, we are sure to strike upon some good English versions that reach on beyond us. Translation ultimately is a deeply creative process. It is a sort of letting go so that the transparency of the original comes back.

No matter what, communicating across borders is extremely challenging. How does one render culturally specific tropes? There are some Punjabi figures of speech that do not make any sense in English. For instance a vital emotional center in Punjabi is *kaleja* (liver), and to a culture that only knows the heart as the seat of emotions, how to communicate that *"kaleje da tukra,"* literally "slice of one's liver," denotes a sweetheart? Furthermore, there are many words with rich topographical associations that are impossible to transport across continents. When Heer, the heroine of Waris Shah's romance, beats up Kaido like a *khes*, the pleasure for the native reader in seeing the nasty fellow being thrashed is augmented by the delightful world conveyed by the word *khes*. Since this cotton blanket is used only when the weather is not too hot nor too cold, it immediately transports Punjabis to those balmy nights spent on the terrace under the starry skies with a cool breeze blowing from the adjoining Thar Desert. Likewise, *churi* technically is a mixture of bread, butter, and molasses, but for the Punjabis it spells a whole lot more – the gooey love of mothers and grandmothers that melt its ingredients.

There are yet other Punjabi terms like *kure*, *ni*, *ve*, *ji*, which have no equivalents whatsoever. *Kure* is an extremely rustic Punjabi term used for girls/women, and I was pleasantly surprised to find it in Bullhe Shah's verse (it is rarely found in written Punjabi and I had not even heard it since my childhood days in Bathinda). A more common term is *ni*, another colloquial term for a woman, which vibrantly flows in the lyrics of our male poets. The masculine equivalent is *ve*, which permeates the work of the poetess Amrita Pritam. These terms coming from the lips of both male and female poets, represent a verbal embrace gushing from the point closest to their unconscious. The male poets addressing the female or the female addressing the male does not indicate a dualistic opposition between *the two genders,* but in Mikhail Bakhtin's term, a "dialogic" relation which is rooted in an openness that leads to a deeper self-awareness, to a deeper communion. Another expression that is ubiquitous in the original is *ji*. As a mark of respect, Punjabis add the suffix "*ji*" to a person's name, but in contrast to the rustic terms *ve* and *ni*, it is a formal and polite form of speech. How to convey these tiny words loaded with such emotive significance? Repetitions (*sun sun*/hearing hearing) and pairs of echo-words (*gup-shup*/"gossip-shossip") are also common in Punjabi, but they sound awkward in English.

And the most challenging of all, how does one translate the abundance of Punjabi synonyms for "love" – *ishq, pyar, muhabbat, bhakti, sneh, rang, prem, prit, cau, neh*…! English language is an utter pauper when it comes to the expressions for love.

Again, those essential hermeneutic principles help out: a genuine respect for both languages, and an openness to new possibilities. When we respect the original and English as equals, the fluidity of sound and sense, and the emotional thrill or anguish, flows between them quite naturally. We therefore need to make a conscious attempt to break away from the homogenized "glob*latin*ized" translations that have dominated the indigenous Indian languages. We can do away with many of those archaic phrases identified by Yeats: "polyglot phrases, sedentary distortions of unnatural English... muddles, muddied by 'Lo! Verily', and 'Forsooth'…"[20]

And we must balance the one-sided androcentric attitudes prevailing the English translations. Neither must we submit to the superiority of His Master's Voice and His cliched rhymes, nor to any extraneous archaic and androcentric impositions. Once we have the space and freedom to think afresh, we create new verbal encounters that can transmit the authenticity and vitality of the original.

In fact, English is an immensely rich language, which touches Punjabi in many tender ways. If we try to stay as close as possible to the original verse, and follow its movements, rhythms, and syntax, Punjabi verse lends itself quite well to English. In this case, Walter Benjamin's popularly quoted thesis that "Languages are not strangers to one another, but are, a priori and apart from all historical relationships, interrelated in what they want to express" rings true.[21] Benjamin's ideal of the interlinear translation in which the translator goes for the literal rendering of the syntax rather than for the semantic content of sentences brings out the equality of Punjabi and English. When we focus on finding the meaning of each word in the original, the semantic prejudices and hegemonies of the "colonial" English have a tougher time penetrating. In the interlinear mode the two languages are literally parallel and so they come face to face as equals. This is the model I have tried to follow.

Since the literary output of these poets is enormous, a very difficult part was to select their works. I tried to take just a few samples from each of them – which I admit was an arduous feat. I have included a few more works by Pritam with a view to maintain the gender balance of my collection. Rather than including one or two poems from numerous Punjabi poets, I wanted to focus on the most representative ones, and give a good feel for their literary styles and mental landscapes, and therefore make it easier for readers to identify with their works. I have interspersed my introductions to the poets in each section with a few short samples in Punjabi, with the hope that my readers will get a taste of the unique aesthetic flavors saturating the original.

An anthology gathering the muse of Sikhs, Muslims, and Hindus is an important example of the collective identity of the people. There are over a hundred million Punjabi speakers worldwide, and in some areas of the United Kingdom and Canada, Punjabi is the second most spoken language after English. The Punjabis today may be religiously divided and they may be politically divided, but the lyrical writings from the Punjab belong to all the communities equally. The Sikh Guru Nanak, the Muslim Waris Shah, the Hindu Dhani Ram Chatrik absorbed the diverse natural, historical, cultural, and social elements of the common Punjabi soil. These poets fabulously illustrate that art, like love, does not have any race or religion or caste or pedigree: "When beauty strikes/Everybody adopts it as their own" ("Qutab Minar"). I hope the Punjabis from both India and Pakistan, and those who have migrated farther to the UK, America, Canada, Africa, and Australia will find this volume meaningful. As Chatrik claims, *boli hai Punjabi sadi* (our language is Punjabi), *jind jan sadi* (our life and breath), *motian di khan sadi* (our treasure of pearls), *hathon nahin guani* (we must not let her slip away from our hands). Language constitutes our identity, our physicality, our very being.

These lyrics from the other side of the world can inform our thinking in the West too, and strengthen our "patchwork heritage." As President Obama reminded us in his historic inaugural address, "we are shaped by every language and culture, drawn from every end of this Earth…" It was inspiring to hear a secular poet at his inauguration; it was inspiring to hear him in Cairo cite the holy Qur'an. Poetry – sacred and secular, from east or west – is calligraphy that spells out our human bond.

1

POETRY FROM SIKH SCRIPTURE

From the many different Gurus and saints gathered in the Guru Granth, I chose Guru Nanak, Guru Arjan, Sheikh Farid, Bhagat Namdev and Bhagat Ravidas. As I have acknowledged, they may be few in number, but they provide a strong feel for the diversity and rich literary textures of the archetypal Punjabi anthology.

Guru Nanak

We will begin with Guru Nanak because it is his vision and syntax that form the base for the entire volume. Nanak reveled in calling himself a poet: "*sasu masu sabhu jio tumara tu mai khara piara / nanaku sairu eva kahatu hai sace parvadgara* – to you belong my breath, to you my flesh; says the poet Nanak, you the True One are my Beloved" (GG: 660). He uses the term *sairu/shair*, which comes from the Arabic word for poetry (*al-shi'r*). S.H. Nasr traces its root meaning to consciousness and knowledge.[1] Guru Nanak's ideal of poetry is therefore very different from our word "poetry," which means making. Rather than making or crafting, the poet Nanak is so consumed by his intense awareness and love for the Divine that he has no control over his words: "*jaisi mai ave khasam ki bani taisara kari gianu ve lalo* – as comes to me the Husband's word, that is what I say O' Lalo!" (GG: 722)

There is very little biographical documentation on him. From popular narratives we learn that he was born in Talwandi, a small village in northern India (now in Pakistan) into a Hindu home. But he rejected social structures and spent his time communing with nature. Later he went to live with his sister Nanaki and her husband Jairam in Sultanpur, and worked at the local grocery shop. It is believed that at Sultanpur Nanak had a revelatory experience into the unicity of the Divine. Thereafter he traveled extensively spreading his vision of the One and its social implications, the oneness of humanity. During most of his travels, his Muslim companion Mardana played on a *rabab*, while Guru Nanak sang songs of intense love addressing the ultimate One in everyday Punjabi. The Sikh Guru's words and the Muslim Mardana's music are intrinsically bonded. The simple style of Guru Nanak's teaching drew people from different religious and social backgrounds. Those who accepted him as their "guru" and followed his teachings came to be known as Sikhs, a Punjabi word which means disciple or seeker (Sanskrit *shishya*; Pali *sekha*).[2]

Guru Nanak's entire teaching is in the poetic mode. Plato may have found poetry too captivating and therefore banished the poets from his Republic, but the divinely inspired Guru tried to awaken his followers and revitalize their senses, psyche, imagination, and spirit through poetry. Martin Heidegger's perspective illuminates the importance of the poetic mode inaugurated by Guru Nanak. For Heidegger, human existence rests and builds upon poetry, and almost quoting Shelley he says, "Language itself is poetry in the essential sense."[3] "Poetry…is not an aimless imagining of whimsicalities and not a flight of mere notions and fancies into the realm of the unreal. What poetry, as illuminating projection, unfolds of unconcealedness and projects ahead into the design of the figure, is the Open which poetry lets happen, and indeed in such a way that only now, in the midst of beings, the Open brings beings to shine and ring out."[4]

Guru Nanak's sonorous verse recorded in the Guru Granth comes in a gusty speed, and taking on beautiful artistic designs, it "lets happen." As we heard him above, the Guru repeatedly points to the Divine as the source of his orality: "*ta mai kahia kahanu ja tujhai kahaia* – I said only what you made me say" (GG: 566). Again, "*hau apahu boli na janda mai kahia sabhu hukmao jio* – language I don't know, I say what you order me to" (GG: 763). The Guru is not following any models nor working to compose his words, and yet his inspired words speedily flow out in perfect rhythm, alliteration, assonance, and consonance! In turn his geometric patterns, verbal arabesques, and linguistic somersaults, awaken the consciousness to the infinite reality permeating each and all. His words coming from a transcendent soil project every bit on earth with meaning – be it a tiny ant or a blade of grass or a fish, so what is overlooked and concealed "shines and rings out" with transcendent joy. The disclosure happens in the moment now – not before or hereafter, and in relationships with others – not in isolation or renunciation. Nanak's language opens the door to a heightened mode of being. Definitely not an aimless or fanciful flight, his poetry is a real feel for the divine vibrancy present everywhere – motivating people to live socially, politically, and spiritually engaged with their families and communities. Guru Nanak's verse has generated one of the five world religions, with more than 23 million people relying on its existential power. For the eminent Sikh historian Harbans Singh, "His genius was best expressed in the poetical attitude. No other way would have been adequate to the range and depth of his mood…"[5]

Guru Nanak's boundless imagination and subtle aesthetic sensitivity served as the paradigm for the Fifth Guru who compiled the 1,430-paged volume for his growing Sikh community. Each of Guru Nanak's compositions poetically expresses his theological vision of the Divine. The volume opens with his statement *Ikk Oan Kar* (One Being Is), and the rest can be read as an artistic hermeneutics of this primal expression of expansiveness and unity. Nanak grew up in a culturally and religiously rich North India with Sufis and Saints from many different orders and schools of thought. In his lifetime, he witnessed Babur's conquest of the relatively peaceful regime of the Muslim Lodi Sultans and the establishment of the Mughal Empire. Nanak's works disclose the common spirituality of his milieu, just as they disclose the prevailing stereotypical binaries: the upper class Brahmin vs. the low Shudra, the Hindu vs. the Muslim. In a sociopolitical context where God was named as either *ram* or *rahim*, the worship was either *namaz* or *puja,* the place of worship *mandir* or *masjid*, and the language of scripture either Sanskrit or Arabic, Guru Nanak proclaimed "1 Being Is." Here the primary numeral "1" common to people of all languages and cultures is followed by the alpha of the Gurmukhi script (also a sign for *Oan*, the primordial Sanskrit syllable *Aum* or Being) and is completed by the sign for Kar (Is), a geometrical arc reaching away into space. While the former two constitute the beginning of the mathematical and verbal languages, the arc is at once without beginning or end. Nanak's fundamental principle gestures motion and movement – an entry into countless possibilities. If the Muslim poet Firoz Din Sharaf admires the Sikh Guru for his ability to explain Vedic and Qur'anic terms (in his poem entitled "Defeated"), it is because he comprehended Guru Nanak's language of Absoluteness and Infinity.

As I have been writing all along, we must not confine Guru Nanak's innovative configuration of *Ikk Oan Kar* to any preexisting molds: the standard translation "There is One God" does not quite express the vastness, the plenitude, or the intimacy bursting forth in the original "One Being Is."[6] Instead of an opening into limitless possibilities as envisioned by the founder Sikh Guru, scholars and translators have selected and structured and shaped *Ikk Oan Kar* into an intimidating male God. As the feminist philosopher Mary Daly reminds us, the term "god" is a reified "noun", which is static and laden with Jewish and Christian patriarchal assumptions. "God" with its "Father-Lord" connotations has negative effects on society as it produces an unhealthy experience with the Divine, and unhealthy relationships amongst people, she writes.[7] Transcending languages, cultures, and religions, Guru Nanak's primary numeral 1 with its soaring geometric arc is a universal modality. In any translation, the 1-ness of the numeral must be retained, and I would say "Be-ing" (recommended by Mary Daly in a Western context) works out quite well as its English equivalent for it preserves Nanak's intention.[8] When his language is accessed directly without patriarchal interpreters and translated without imperial hegemonies, its liberating enchantment becomes existentially available to those who hear him.

There is no need for adding the term "soul" in English translations either. Sikh scripture permeates with words like *sakhi* (female friend), *suhagan* (bride) *nar, mahal, and kaman* (all three denoting woman). But whenever these original words are translated, the term "soul" somehow gets latched on. Laden with Jewish-Christian connotations, "soul" is not appropriate in the Sikh context. It imposes a mind-body dualism that devalues bodies, female gender and sexuality, and shifts the attention from life on earth here and now to an afterlife and heaven out there. A simple *suhagan* (bride) for example, becomes "bride-soul." The addition reduces the robust and authentic presence of female scriptural models into a mere figure of speech. It sends misogynistic and geophoebic messages to readers.

The essential celebration of the Divine One at the outset is followed by Guru Nanak's composition called the Japuji (*japu* signifies quiet prayer, and *ji* is the Punjabi suffix for respect). Since this inaugural hymn of the Guru Granth forms the core of Sikh ethics and metaphysics, I have included it in its entirety. Devotees recite Japuji at the break of dawn, "the ambrosial hour," considered most conducive to grasping its poetic force. While its prologue affirms the existence of the infinite One, its 38 stanzas celebrate the vibrancy of the cosmos reverberating with That singular Divine. Its vivid descriptions make readers feel a part of a magical plurality consisting of different complexions, faiths, heroes, rituals, languages, and species (Japuji: 27).

Towards the finale, readers are launched on a five-fold spiritual journey – across the realms of *Dharam, Gyan, Saram, Karam and Sach* (Duty,

Knowledge, Beauty, Action, and Truth). As the journey progresses into wider planes and deeper depths, we come face to face with the infinity we partake in: "Here are continents, constellations, and universes, whose limits cannot be told" (Japuji: 37). The epilogue of the hymn presents a memorable scene in which the "entire universe" (sagal jagat) with its variegated and complex multiplicity "plays" (khele) in the lap of "day and night, the two female and male nurses" (divas rati dui dai daia). This first poem of the Granth constitutes a remarkably organic textual body: its prologue introduces the infinity of Be-ing; its epilogue vividly depicts humans and nature cozily nestled together on the Body of That metaphysical One.

Guru Nanak's hymn entitled "Arati" is also very popular. It is recited by Sikhs every evening as they reverently close their holy book and put it to rest for the night. In some shrines it is an enormously festive event. At the Golden Temple for instance, the Arati sung by the congregation sonorously fills the air as the Guru Granth is taken in a gold and silver palanquin (palki) from the central shrine for its nightly rest, and the devotees (and visitors) in a procession take turns – offering their shoulders – to carry the revered Book. The hymn celebrates the cosmic choreography of the planets, and like the Japuji, it puts us in touch with something much larger. This joyous hymn is often interpreted as a repudiation of the traditional Hindu custom in which devotees encircle a platter with lamps, incense, and fruit around their favorite deities. In fact, Nanak's Arati recounts the spacious and ethereal skies as the platter (thal) on which the sun, moon and twinkling starry lamps perform arati around the infinite One. In his poetic leap, entire vegetation comes together as a bouquet offered in homage, and the breeze blows from and in all directions as the fragrant incense. Rather than split Sikh from Hindu, Nanak's discourse invites everybody – Hindus, Muslims, Jews, Christians, and Sikhs to hear and see and rejoice in the cosmic harmony. Instead of its interpreters, it is the text that needs to be heard directly.

By designating the Divine as numeral "1" Nanak shattered the dominance of conventional male motifs and divisive categories; he opened up a space for the Divine to be experienced in other new and important ways. So he and his successor Gurus reveal countless ways of imagining and experiencing that infinite One. In Guru Nanak's compositions, we see the Divine as the bride in her wedding dress, as the groom on the nuptial bed... as the fisherman and the fish, as the waters and the trap, as the weight holding the net, as well as the lost ruby swallowed by the fish. In a speedy tempo, his similes and paradoxes free the mind from narrow walls. His literary tropes parallel natural phenomena: just as in nature new qualities can be engendered by the coming together of elements in new ways, so too, new semantic juxtapositions and combinations can produce a new *isness*.[9] Is the Divine the dressed up bride or the groom on the nuptial bed? Breaking out of ordinary linear thought, Nanak's language makes way for a new dimension of reality and being in this world. The artist offers readers myriad possibilities of recollecting the infinite One – without letting the mind halt on any one. It is also noteworthy that nothing in the cosmos is polluted or deemed too low for the Divine to sparkle through. Humans are not the only ones endowed with spiritual treasures – the fish has swallowed the ruby too!

Guru Arjan

Like his predecessor, the Fifth Guru heard language flowing out of a transcendent hub: "*agam agocaru sacu sahibu mera nanaku bolai bolaia tera* – unfathomable, ineffable, truth is my sovereign; Nanak speaks what you want him to" (GG: 743).[10] A spontenous expression of the ontological force of the universe, speaking here is free from conceptual webs and linguistic codifications. Adhering to Guru Nanak's discourse, Guru Arjan reiterates the singularity of that source: "Some call it Rama, some call it Khuda; some worship it as Vishnu, some as Allah" (GG: 885). In order to crystallize the founder Guru's universal vision for perpetuity, he collected the verses of the Sikh Gurus, Hindu Bhagats, and Muslim saints from different social and geographical backgrounds. Through his profound personal sensibility, Guru Arjan heard the essential human language; he did not get stuck on external differences in accents, intonations, grammar, vocabulary or imagery.

He certainly did not aim at a blend of Hindu-Muslim ideas, for that would only deny the rich distinctions he respected. Till very recently books on world religions categorized Sikhism as a prime example of synthesis or "syncretism."[11] Such presumptions fail to see the originality of the Sikh poetic horizon. Guru Arjan did not try to add two disparate traditions to reproduce a hybrid Sikh text; he did not assemble their passages and market it as a new product. What he did seek was a vertical expansion of the spiritual consciousness shared by Hindus, Muslims, and Sikhs. And what he created was a literary text scripted in an enduring relationship with people of other faiths.

That the Sikh Guru voluntarily and consciously chose to incorporate the different religious paradigms of his day into the Sikh sacred volume shows his unusually liberal attitude. This inclusive process of textual compilation had begun early on. As textual historians Gurinder Singh Mann and Pashaura Singh have shown, two extant manuscripts (known as the *Goindval Pothis*) prepared by Guru Arjan's maternal grandfather, Guru Amar Das (Nanak 3) contain 129 hymns by non-Sikh saints. It was important for the Sikh Gurus that people would familiarize themselves with difference and diversity. The "other" could not merely be tolerated; the "other" had to be engaged with, understood, and appreciated. So in the making of Sikh scripture, Guru Arjan collected the voices of Sikh, Muslim, and Hindu poets and gave them equal status. He even set their poetry into musical measures so readers and hearers could aesthetically experience That One conceived in different forms and expressed in different styles. The pluralistic spectrum was important for the intellectual, emotional and spiritual development of his religiously diverse society. The Fifth made Guru Nanak's ideal of the singular Divine into a concrete reality.

This compiler of the Granth was also a superb poet, and 2,218 of the hymns are by him. Guru Arjan articulates his passion for the divine One in a way that brings together the two religious "opposites" of his day most naturally. Strikingly similar to the Punjabi Sufi poets we will be reading in the next chapter, he categorically rejects institutional forms of religion. He says he will neither keep the Hindu fasts nor will he fast during the holy month of Ramadan. He will not make pilgrimage either to the Hindu sacred spots or to the Ka'ba. He will not perform *puja* or *namaz*. He is neither Hindu nor Muslim. Paradoxical though it may sound, these negations build up to construct the strongest and most positive assertion of Guru Arjan's inclusive belief in the singular Divine "*ek gusain allah mera* – the One is my Gusain and Allah." His acceptance of these two mutually exclusive categories of his day ("Hindu" *Gusian* and "Muslim" *Allah*) shows tremendous confidence and courage on the part of the poet. He ardently serves the One: "*eko sevai avar na duja* – I serve the One and no other." And he celebrates, "I am the body and breath of Allah and Ram – *allah ram ke pind pran!*" What could be more palpable, more vital, more effective than his diction? In the final verse of this hymn Guru Arjan acknowledges Bhagat Kabir who had made a similar assertion. As the very body (*pind*) and breath (*pran*) of Allah and Ram, the Sikh Guru needed no formal rituals or categories to buttress his faith in That One. It perfectly shows his intimacy with the divine One beyond borders of any sort. While their society was rife with conflict between the followers of Allah or

Ram/Gusain, the Guru Granth poets were enchanted with the Divine and expressed it so.

Furthermore, this infinite One is intimately experienced as *both* male and female: *"ape purakh ape hi nar* – itself male, itself is female" (GG: 1020). In a socio-historic context that was extremely patriarchal, he pronounces *"tun mera pita tun hain mera mata* – You are my father, you are my mother" (GG: 103; GG: 1144); with a slight variation, *"tumhi pita tum hi phun mata* – you are my father and you too are my mother" (GG: 1215), and yet again, *"mat pita bandhap tun hai tun sarab nivas* – you are our mother, father, relative, and you permeate us all" (GG: 818). In these emotionally charged verses he embraces the transcendent abiding in everybody in a range of family figures. The sense of plenitude strips off patriarchal stratifications. It blots out masculine identity as the norm for imaging the Divine, and widens the spiritual experience.

The compiler Guru intended his community to gain supreme enjoyment from the literary volume. Once the materials were gathered, he set most of them into the ancient Indian musical system of Ragas (*raga* means both "color" and "musical mode" in Sanskrit). This enormous task required amazing effort and knowledge on his part. The revealed word empowered by the *raga-s* in turn serves as a melodious instrument for stimulating the faculties for intuiting the Divine.

Along with the sense of hearing, the Guru made tasting vitally important for divine cognition and enjoyment. In his epilogue (*mundavani*) to the Guru Granth he specifies his objective:

> *thal vicu tinu vastu paio sat santokh vicaro…*
> *je ko khavai je ko bhuncai tis ka hoe udharo*

> On the platter lie three things:
>   Truth, contentment, reflection…
> They who eat, they who savor,
>   They are liberated.

Most often philosophers and theologians view food and drink as antithesis to seeing, knowledge, and morality. Sensed by the tongue, bounded to bodies, and associated with the force of appetite, eating is theoretically disdained. But the language of eating and drinking sumptuously pervades the Guru Granth. For his finale, Guru Arjan has used an appetizing analogy. The sacred volume is a *thal* (large metal dish) holding the food of truth (*sat*), contentment (*santokh*), and reflection (*vicar*). The identity of knowledge and food lodged here in Guru Arjan's epilogue is actually prefigured in Guru Nanak's opening hymn: *"bhugati gianu daia bhandarani –* knowledge (*gianu*) is the spread (*bhugati*); compassion (*daia*), the hostess (*bhandarani*)" (Japuji: 29); and as we just saw, it is configured in his cosmic platter performing Arati to the infinite One. The first Guru integrally connected knowledge with compassion: without immersion into the human condition, what good is the intellect? It would be a banquet table spread with dishes without anybody partaking. Compassion dissolves the self-centered ego into a warm hospitality, which tends towards others. The dishes implicit in Guru Nanak's spread are specified by Guru Arjan as truth (*sat*), contentment (*santokh*), and reflection (*vicar*). Though they are made up of epistemological ingredients, these dishes are not intellectually conceived or logically argued; they are swallowed and digested by the body in the company of others. Guru Arjan's language creates new mental networks. As the conceptual knowledge of the absolute reality, Truth (*sat*) flows in two directions: coming inwards, it gathers joy and contentment for the individual (*santokh*, from the Sanskrit *sam*/together and *tush*/happy or content), and it spreads out towards others (*vicar* from the Sanskrit *vi*/out or spread and *c'ar*/go). By offering the Guru Granth as a platter, Guru Arjan draws attention to the sapiential quality of divine knowledge that is personally fulfilling and must be shared and reflected upon with others.

However, simple eating (*khavai*) is not enough; the aesthetic heightening, savoring (*bhuncai*), is vital for him. Cognitive and sensuous faculties dynamically fuse in the process of savoring. The sense of sight was lauded by the ancient Vedic seers (*vid*/to see) as the supreme faculty, and judged as the "higher" sense by Plato and Kant.[12] Whereas sight retains a gap between the object of knowledge and the perceiving subject, the sense of taste overcomes any distance by intimately bringing the "other" into the very body of the percipient. For the Guru Granth poets, the oral is the aural. Guru Arjan equates language (*bani*) with ambrosia (*amrit*), and qualifies it as delicious essence (*amio rasa*; GG: 963). *Rasa* is a crucial term in Indian aesthetics, incorporating qualities and experiences common to food and arts. Literally the juice of plants, *rasa* is the refined essence of an object, its taste or flavor, the relishing by the taster, a cultivated sensibility, and a base for many sophisticated theories.[13] In the Guru Granth, the organ of tongue is literally *rasana*. *"Amrit bani rasana chakhai* – my tongue tastes the ambrosial language," divulges Guru Arjan (GG: 395). His use of *rasa* evokes the elemental nutrients of sacred poetry and importantly, their awareness and appreciation. Thus the Guru brings about a shift from the object to the subject, from the divine word to its human reception, from knowing to savoring.

Language from the beyond is succulently sipped: "*tapati bujhani amrit bani tripte jio barik kheer* – as milk quenches the child, ambrosial *bani* quenches all heat" (GG: 978). The physical and psychological sustenance provided by mother's milk conjoins with the spiritual growth derived from the sacred verse. The Guru joyously recalls the experience of "her milk in a baby's mouth – *jaisay barik mukh kheer*" (GG: 987), and describes the satisfaction and fulfillment that comes with it (GG: 1266). A nourishing maternal metaphor is repeatedly heard in the voice of the Gurus: "says Nanak, the child, you are my father and my mother, and your name is like milk in my mouth – *nanak barik tum mat pita mukh nam tumaro kheera*" (GG: 713). They unabashedly express their attachment to the Divine through an infant's attachment to the mother's breast: "my mind loves the Divine, O my life, like a child loves suckling milk – *har seti man bedhi meri jindurhiai jio balak lag dudh kheerai ram*" (GG: 538). Like the maternal milk, words fill the mouth. Palpable in the mouth, language and drinking are both sensuous experiences.

The poetry Guru Arjan gathered is the tactile articulation of words no different from the dishes of truth, contentment, and reflection, the spread on the banquet hosted by compassion, the platter in the hands of the cosmos, the mother's nutritious breast milk. Such is its force that "hearing it brings joy to mind and body – *sun sun man tan haria*" (GG: 781). Once drenched in its passion, its color never leaves or fades (GG: 427). The sacred and the secular, the metaphysical and the physical, the Divine and the human are not separate at all. The transcendent is actualized in the daily human acts of hearing, speaking, tasting.

Sheikh Farid

The rich ingredients of the literary platter offered by Guru Arjan for his growing Sikh community come not only from Sikh Gurus but also from Muslim and Hindu saints. Our next poet is Sheikh Farid (1175–1265). Two of his hymns are placed in Rag Asa (GG: 488), two in Rag Suhi (GG: 794), and his collection of couplets comes toward the end of the Guru Granth (pp. 1377–84). There are also several passages where the Sikh Gurus are in conversation with the Sufi saint. Throughout his haunting poetry, Sheikh Farid articulates moral and philosophical ideals of Sufism. He addresses the One as Khuda, Allah, and Rabb, and his verse is imbued with Sufi patterns and Qur'anic allusions. The Muslim saint etches the imagination with the figure of a genuine dervish tightly fastened to the robe of the utterly transcendent Divine! We hear him exalt mothers who give birth to such devotees. In another hymn he tellingly uses the maternal metaphor to remind us of the transience of life: whereas it takes nine months for humans to form in the mother's womb, it takes a mere instant to die!

The angel of death and the fear of judgment are always hovering in his poetry. Much as we may stay alert with our eyes wide open, the angel of death sneaks in, "extinguishing the two lamps on his way out – *divre gaia bujhae*" (48). The introduction of Azrail leads the reader towards Islamic theology. Birds too – cranes, crows, egrets, swans and hawks – mournfully point to the finality of death. As the birds hatch their young ones in the skeletal sockets (14), they graphically illustrate the eventual decay of the vibrant human body. In his constant reminders of death and the Day of Judgment, Sheikh Farid is close to his contemporary West Asian Sufis. As Annemarie Schimmel comments on the early Sufis:

> Even though Paradise and Hell did not matter to the devotees of mystical love, they were well aware that their deeds would bear fruit, and one of the favorite sayings attributed to the Prophet was constantly repeated by the moderate mystics: "This world is seedbed for the Otherworld."[14]

The flux of life is juxtaposed to the eternal Allah, so death and decay are transcended through love for the Divine. Sheikh Farid admires the pitch-black koel-bird perched amongst the mango trees. Painfully aware of the absence of her transcendent Allah, her vibrancy and joy are taken over by the heavy dye of dark agony. Yet the notes of the charred koel-bird are buoyant: if there is compassion, she will have her passionate union.

Sheikh Farid's admiration extends to all those birds in the forest that live in solitude, feed on pebbles, and while perched on sandy dunes, constantly remember the Divine. Such verses disclose Sheikh Farid's ascetic orientation. He lived the Sufi path and promoted abstinence and arduous practices which would bring about spiritual purification. As an early Sufi, he was maintaining the pattern of his contemporaries for whom "the *sharia* proclaimed in the Qur'an and exemplified by the Prophet together with a firm belief in the Day of Judgment, was the soil out which their piety grew."[15] Schimmel further acknowledges that Sheikh Farid performed rigorous ascetic practices, including "the *chilla ma'kusa*, hanging upside down in a well and performing the prescribed prayers and recollections for forty days." Legend has it that Sheikh Farid was miraculously rewarded for his fasting, as pebbles turned to stone, therefore he is popularly called Ganj-i shakar ("granary of sugar").[16] Below we have Farid's own poetic testament. In his intense love for Allah, he performed such severe austerities that his self is completely annihilated; his blood is transformed into love:

> *farida rati rat na niklai je tan chirai koe*
> *jo tan rate rabe sio tin tan rat na hoe*

> Not a drop of blood would spill
>   If my body were cut; says Farid,
> Those who are imbued in love for Rabb,
>   Their bodies are devoid of blood. (51)

The overall sadness of Sheikh Farid's consciousness and his asceticism form quite a contrast to the exuberance of the Sikh Gurus who valued life and living. Spiritual liberation for Arjan is attained "in the midst of laughing, playing, dressing up, and eating – *hasandia khelandia painandia khavandia viche hovai mukt*" (GG: 522). The differences continue. Whereas the mother's breasts flow with invigorating milk in the Sikh Gurus' poetry, they are withered and dried up in Farid's hymn. Over and again the young woman we meet in Guru Nanak's or Guru Arjan's verse is fragrant with the perfume of divine name but in Sheikh Farid's hymn we encounter the ignorant woman who "stinks of asafetida." Native to Iran, this herb with a pungent smell is used extensively in Indian cooking. Indeed, Sheikh Farid's West Asian sensibilities enlarge and spice up Guru Arjan's poetic platter. Even more so, their incorporation in the Sikh sacred text reveals profound respect for the faith of others. Sheikh Farid's religious prescriptions, his rigorous asceticism, his intense anxiety in this world, his fear of judgment, his eschatological perspectives are all so different from that of the Sikh Gurus. Yet, they are consciously included in the Sikh sacred book with full acknowledgement of their distinctiveness and difference. There are even several scriptural instances where the Sikh Gurus (Nanak, Amar Das and Arjan) directly respond to and enter dialogue with the Muslim Sheikh.[17] We have here a fine example of an active and meaningful engagement with diversity.

Sheikh Farid does share with the Sikh Gurus the respect for every person, and a fundamental longing for the Divine. "Every heart is a delicate jewel – *sabhna man manik*," so "if you desire your beloved, do not hurt anyone – *je tao piria di sik hiao na thahe kahi da*" (130). Love for the Divine is not a self-centered obsession; rather, it imbues the person with sensitivity and tenderness towards all those around them. Sheikh Farid's moral instruction cuts across religion, sex, class and creed. His rural informal discourse further highlights his poetic affinity with the Sikh Gurus. To this day Punjabis love sweets and rich creamy buffalo milk, so says Farid, "*sakar khand nivat gur makhio manjha dudh sabhai vastu mithian* – brown sugar, white sugar, rock candy, molasses, honey, creamy buffalo milk – these are all sweet things…." However mouthwatering, "*rabb na pujan tudhu* – O Rabb, none come close to you!" (27) As we found sapiential quality of knowledge was extremely important in the verse of the Gurus. Truth was not an ontological or epistemological fact; that One has to be tasted and felt and made a part of the self and extended towards fellow beings. The Sikh literary platter is filled with the devout Muslim's rich delicacies so readers would expand their aesthetic and moral sensibilities. In recognition of his impact, "Sheikh Baba Farid Chair" was established at the Punjab University in Chadigarh in 1976 to promote the study of Punjabi Sufi poetry.

Bhagat Namdev

Similarly, the Bhakats add their own special spiritual ingredients. They too image the Divine but from their polyphonic Hindu imagination, they offer a different hue and vibrancy. They too protest against the ancient caste system, untouchability, religious divisions, and basic human degradation, but because many of them were born in the lowest rung of society, they provide a personal perspective, which is extremely compelling. Now their language is not Punjabi as such: Namdev was from Maharashtra; Ravidas was from Benares. However their crisp style, novel idioms, and universal themes are familiar to all Punjabis. Some have even become a part of the daily parlance. These "Hindu" poets speaking in a mixture of Hindi (Khari Boli of Delhi region), Rajasthani or Punjabi are appropriated in the classic Punjabi text, the Guru Granth, and are integral to it.

In his innovative cultural history of Bhagat Namdev (*Religion and Public Memory*), Christian Lee Novetzke offers interesting snippets circulating about the life of the saint over the last seven centuries. Namdev or Nama (as we hear him call himself in his poetry) grew up an impoverished family of calico printers in the vicinity of the pilgrimage center of Pandharpur in the Marathi speaking region of the Deccan. For the Hindu theistic community of the *Varkaris* (meaning pilgrims), this was an important spiritual centre. The Varkaris are worshippers of Vishnu and his incarnations. Bhagat Namdev became the foundational figure of this large and ancient religious sect of the south. He also travelled widely in north

India, and a network of shrines and memorials became associated with him. His inclusion in the Guru Granth and his wide travels have given Namdev a multilingual multireligious pan-Indian cosmopolitan image. In the modern period it was reinforced to project him as *rashtriya sant* – saint for the new nation of India. Novetzke describes the nationalists reinventing the Hindu Namdev as a secular humanist who champions the low caste, the poor, and the oppressed, and as a unifier of Hindus and Muslims. He even quotes the former Prime Minister of India Indira Gandhi praise Namdev as "one of the foremost" teachers of the Bhakti movement who "rescued our society in the Mediaeval Period from total subservience to ritual and the rigours of the caste system."[18]

Namdev's own verse leaves us with an intimate feel for his personality and his milieu. We can see the smile on his face and hear the bounce in his gait as he comes to worship in the temple: "*hasat khelat tere dehure aia* – laughing and playing I entered your door" – only to be forcefully grabbed and driven out (GG: 1164). Namdev's ensuing dialogue with the divine concretizes the utter hopelessness of his situation: "*hinri jati meri jadim raia chhipe ke janam kahe kau aia* – my caste is terribly low, O king of Yadavs! Why was I born into a family of calico printers?" The fact that the low caste person imagines God as a high caste (*Yadav*) king (*raia*) indicates the social and cultural grounding of the poet. Poetry is not a whimsical flight; it embodies everyday life. As Namdev's rhetorical question rises from the bottom of his humiliation, it poignantly captures his caste-based social oppression and ostracization. All that horrible discrimination just because of biological birth (*janam*) that he had no choice in? He doesn't fight back. He says nothing bitter. Instead, we see him picking up his blanket and walking out to sit at the back of the temple. In his three-dimensional autobiographical representation, we can fully identify with the saint and empathize with him. (Namdev has much in common with the twentieth-century women protagonists in Amrita Pritam's works we enounter in the final chapter.) But the force of his love turned the temple around to face him! Namdev's emphasis on the inwardness of religiosity and his total infatuation with the Divine emerges brilliantly. The motion of his simple words creates a wheel of images with emotional and spiritual resonance for the reader. We can understand why he would continue to attract followers who perpetuate his teachings and revere him as their guru.

There are 60 hymns of Namdev in the Guru Granth, and we hear in them his critique of cultural hegemonies, religious authorities, and external practices (asceticism, yogic exercises, pilgrimages, sacrifices, charities…).

Throughout his verse, Namdev gives priority to the love for the Divine whom he envisions and names in many different ways. The kaleidoscope of images, allusions, and symbols he brings in from his Hindu heritage to express his devotion is an important contribution to the Guru Granth. Just a short poem "I Come To You" for example opens up a vast horizon of classical Indian literature, including the Puranas, the Mahabharata, and the Ramayana. Namdev begins by addressing Vishnu as his father, as the husband of goddess Laxmi, and as his longhaired dark lover. Agape and Eros mingle in his sentiments, as does his imagery of Vishnu, Krishna, and Ram subsequently. Having come to seek refuge, the "untouchable" recalls three significant moments of divine generosity. In the first one Vishnu descends from his paradise to help out the elephant attacked by an angry crocodile. In this Puranic myth, the royal elephant piteously trumpets for help and struggles in vain to free himself from the mouth of the angry crocodile, but as soon as he ardently prays to Vishnu, the lord casts his disc and destroys the enemy, setting his devotee free. In the second, Namdev draws upon the unforgettable scene of the disrobing of Draupadi by the villainous Duhshasana from the great Indian epic Mahabharata. The wife of the heroic Pandava brothers, Draupadi, is dragged by her hair and terribly humiliated in public. At this critical juncture she passionately calls for Krishna, who immediately helps her retain her honor by supplying her with an outfit that keeps on unfurling. Namdev's use of the multivalent term *ambar* (meaning circumference, clothes, sky) projects the heroine being protected by a celestial circle of garments. In the third, Namdev alludes to the narrative of Ahalya, the wife of the Gautama Muni, from the other great Indian epic, the Ramayana. So beautiful was Ahalya that even lord Indra coveted her. One morning, when Gautama had gone for this morning ablutions, Indra disguised himself in his form and made love with Ahalya. When the husband found out he did not empathize with the victim; rather, he blamed Ahalya and turned her into stone with his curse. Ahalya ultimately regained her humanity with the compassionate touch of Lord Ram's foot. The poet identifies with these legendary victims, and aspires to freedom, honor, and humanity by emulating their devotion.

Namdev's literary prism presents many significant historical venues and geographical sites of ancient India. Not only do we see Draupadi in Duhshasana's court, we also get to visit the sacred Hindu city of Kashi and the playful gardens of Brindaban. We meet with Mother Devaki. We get glimpses into Hindu mythology with the world unfolding from a white lotus. We learn about Hindu rituals and the performance of the ancient Vedic Horse Sacrifice. We are introduced to Samkhya philosophy with Purusha's Maya manifesting herself. And we sumptuously hear Krishna's "blessed flute" that seduces each and all. But underlying the universe is the beat of that singular formless (*nirguna*) Ram. Everything stationary, everything moving, be they worms or moths, humans or flowers, elephants or ants, their pulse resounds with that One. The formless is seen in myriad forms (*saguna*). The divine is the formless Ram; the divine is the dark handsome longhaired Krishna performing his dances and music.

The Sikh Gurus did not propagate any theory of incarnation or any mythological notions of creation. In fact the Japuji categorically states that the One cannot be installed into any form; no myth explains when or how creation came to be. Yet, it was the broad-mindedness of the Gurus that drew them to people holding worldviews different from their own. There is a genuine intention to know and interact with people of other faiths and overcome any sense of alienation or fear of the other. Hindu poets like Namdev introduce the indigenous Indian past just as Sufi Sheikh Farid opens readers to the West Asian universe. If Namdev relates to the One in the form of Krishna or Ram there was no reason to exclude him from the Sikh sacred text. Since nothing, nothing whatsoever, could be excluded from the Infinite One envisioned by the founder Sikh Guru, his Fifth successor confidently included the multitude of concepts and images. Namdev's presence in the foremost Punjabi poetry anthology highlights its inherent pluralism, and offers a true understanding of "monotheism."

Bhagat Ravidas

The final poet in this section is Bhagat Ravidas. A tanner and cobbler by birth, he worked with dead animals, which relegated him to the absolute bottom of society. He frequently refers to his low social status and the social discrimination he suffered. But he is the exalted saint in the Guru Granth with 41 hymns inscribed in it. During Sikh death rituals, it is his verse that is recited. As the cortege moves during a person's last journey on earth, they are called upon to recognize and praise the eternal Reality in the voice of Ravidas:

> The day that comes
> That day must go
> Whatever we do
> Won't be forever.

> Our friends departed,
> So must we;
> Long may be the path
> But death hovers above. (GG: 793)

The haunting beauty of this hymn is reminiscent of Sheikh Farid's verse. We must remain cognizant of the fragility and transitory nature of life, and attune ourselves to the infinite Divine. Many other hymns of Bhagat Ravidas are also very popular and sung in Sikh homes and places of worship. Their simplicity and poignancy invariably captivate the psyche.

Like the other Guru Granth poets, Bhagat Ravidas denounces traditional hierarchies and hegemonies of class and caste. He protests against the fourfold division of Indian society into Brahmins, Kshatriyas, Vaishyas, and Shudras, and champions the equality and dignity of all people. His society was obsessed with the notions of purity and pollution, which bolstered the hegemony of the Brahmin class. Untouchables like him – and Namdev – were prohibited from entering temples, celebrating festivals, and from seeing or being seen by the priestly Brahmins. Ravidas is much more trenchant in his critique than Namdev. Utilizing the simplest situations of life, he catches the attention of his readers, and in a host of idioms he makes his biting critiques. The person from the tanner caste knew well what pollution meant. Milk, flowers, and water considered pure are ritually offered to the gods. But says Ravidas,

> The suckling calf
> Polluted the milk,
> Bees polluted the flower,
> And the fish, the water. (GG: 525)

His terse diction strongly ridicules the notions of purity and pollution that were so critical for his society.

He reiterates inwardness as authentic religious experience, which permeates throughout the Guru Granth. Instead of external acts of piety and ceremonial worship, Ravidas offers total devotion to the Divine: "Your Name is the lamp/Your Name is the wick/Your Name is the oil/I pour into it" (GG: 694). Like the Gurus and the Sufis and the rest of the Bhagats, he is passionately attached to the Divine – so tightly bound, that he is free of all others!

In a mystical tone, Ravidas discloses the intimacy between his microcosmic self and the macrocosmic divine. A host of lovely juxtapositions depict their relationship:

> *ja tum divra ta ham bati*
> *ja tum tirath ta ham jati*

> If you are the lamp,
>   I am the wick;
> If you are the sacred spot,
>   I am the pilgrim. (GG: 658)

In another poem Ravidas artistically says "*tohi mohi mohi tohi antaru kaisa* – between you and me and me and you what difference can there be?" (GG: 93) His analogies expressing the human-divine unity are stunning to begin with, and their impact is only augmented by his use of rhetoric. Can the shape of the bracelet be distinguished from the gold? Can the wave be distinguished from the water? His questions powerfully strike the imagination and make us truly wonder. The bracelet and the tiny wave become vividly visible – to the point where the reader is left with only the gold and the boundless sea. The poet sweeps us into a sphere of infinite freedom and ecstasy.

In recent decades Ravidas has gained immense prominence among communities rebelling against caste discrimination and class oppression. He is hailed as a religious and cultural icon in the Punjab, a prophet of the Dalit consciousness, the voice of the Untouchables. His egalitarian values have inspired reform movements like Gandhi's Harijan Sevak Sangh, Dr. Ambedkar's Scheduled Caste Federation, and the Ad Dharam movement in the Punjab. Bhagat Ravidas has also become very popular amongst the Punjabi Dalit diasporic communities. Identifying with the victimization of the medieval saint, the Ravidasis are building their distinctive Gurdwaras. In the UK, they constitute quite a visible community. It is most encouraging that in spite of being stigmatized and discriminated against, the poet would sing of such beauty and hope in the human condition. For Ravidas the relationship between the Divine and human is absolutely necessary; neither can do without the other: "the master is known by the devotee; the devotee, by the master – *parabh te jan janijai jan te suami*" (GG: 93). The poet gives us a glimpse of the supreme power held by the powerless.

From their distinct perspectives, the Guru Granth poets express their desire for the transcendent One. Language indeed is the vital link. In his Japuji Guru Nanak says, "by words we speak and by words we write, by words we communicate and unite" (stanza 19). His multiverse depends upon communication and union, which are brought about by language. The syllables of poetic language are life and life's continuity; its sounds are breath, blood, water, and food. Guru Nanak even praises the tiny sparrow, which joyfully calls for her Divine beloved: "*khudai khudai*" (GG: 1286). What is deeply felt comes out most naturally. The sublime words shift from tongue to tongue. Whatever came spontaneously was quickly uttered, whether it was in Punjabi, Hindi, Braj, Persian, or Arabic. Like the primordial sound of the heartbeat, their verses pulsate with life and vigor. As Bhagat Namdev lyrically asserts, "*sabhai ghat ram bolai ram bolai, ram bina ko bolai re* – in every heart speaks Ram; yes, Ram speaks. Who else would speak other than Ram?" (GG: 988) The desire for the Divine is not the doing of the poets; it is a gift from the Divine.

Of course, the "selection process" on the part of the compiler Guru must have been an incredible challenge. From the vast literary world of medieval India, he tried to select which would best represent Guru Nanak whose vision was boundless to begin with. His choice ends up being perfect. Even those who are well versed in Bhakti and Sufi literature discover something new in the verses enshrined in the Guru Granth. Namdev exalts the wool of the sheep from which his beloved Krishna's shawl is made! The warmth and beauty of such images melt away doctrinal hostilities; their tender strokes sweep away all jagged conflicts between aniconic Islam and representational Hinduism. The scholars and the followers are indebted to Guru Arjan for recording the voice of some of the founding fathers of the Indian religious traditions. The Fifth Guru modeled this valuable archive on Guru Nanak's infinite platter, which holds the sun, the moon, and the fragrant breeze. As a result, his literary platter ends up being equally vast, utterly transcendent, and full of sumptuous delicacies belonging to different ethnicities, castes, and religions. Readers can feed on its nutritious variety, and derive aesthetic pleasure, moral values, psychological calm, and religious understanding.

Guru Nanak

ॐ ॐ

Prelude

There is One Being
Truth is Its Name
Primal Creator
Without fear,
Without enmity
Timeless in form
Unborn
Self-existent
The gift of the Guru.

Japu

Truth before time
Truth within time
Truth here and now
Says Nanak, Truth is evermore.

Thought cannot think it,
    nor will a million thoughts,
Silence cannot silence it,
    nor will seamless contemplation,
Greed is not made greedless,
    not by the wealth of the whole world,
Though a thousand mental feats become a million,
    not one can go with us.

How then to be true?
　　How then to break the wall of lies?
By following the Will,
　　Says Nanak, this is written for us.

2

By the Will, all forms were created;
　　what the Will is, no one can say.
By the Will, all life is formed
　　and by the Will, all are exalted.
The Will determines what is high and what is low;
　　the Will grants all joy and suffering.
Some are blessed by the Will
　　others migrate from birth to birth.
All are within the Will,
　　none stand apart.
Says Nanak, by recognizing the Will,
　　we silence our selfish ego.

3

Those who are filled with might, sing praise of Its might;
Those who recognize the signs, sing praise of Its bounty,
Those who perceive Its virtues, sing praise of Its glory.
Some sing praises through high philosophy;
Some sing praises of Its powers to create and destroy;
Some sing in awe of Its giving and taking of life.
Some sing of Its distance, Its utter transcendence;
Some sing of Its proximity, Its close watch over all.
Stories and stories add one to another,
Preaching and preaching lead nowhere.
The Giver gives, the receivers tire of receiving;
Age upon age they eat and eat Its gifts.
All are directed by Its Will;
Says Nanak, the Carefree is ever in bliss.

4

The True Sovereign, Truth is Its Name,
　　infinite love Its language.

Seekers keep seeking gifts
>   and the Giver gives more and more.
What can we offer for a glimpse of the Court?
What can we say to win Its love?
In the ambrosial hour, exalt and reflect upon the True Name.
Through actions each is dressed in a body;
>   but liberation comes only from Its Gaze.
Says Nanak, know the Absolute thus.

5

It cannot be molded or made,
Itself immaculate and self-existent
Those who serve, receive honors.
Nanak says, sing of the treasure of virtues.
Sing, listen, and hold love in the heart,
So sorrow is banished, joy ushered in.
>   By the Guru, comes the sacred word,
>   by the Guru, comes the scripture,
>   by the Guru, It is experienced in all;
The Guru is Shiva, the Guru is Vishnu, the Guru is Brahma
>   the Guru is Parvati, Laxmi, and Sarasvati.[19]
Were I to comprehend, I'd still fail to explain,
>   for It is beyond all telling.
Guru, let me grasp this one thing:
All creatures have one Provider
>   – may I never forget!

6

I would bathe at a pilgrimage spot only to please that One,
>   without approval what is the use?
I see the expanse of creation,
>   how could it be without Its favor?
Hearing a single teaching from the Guru,
>   jewels, rubies, and pearls begin to shine in the mind.
Guru, let me grasp this one thing:
All creatures have one Provider
>   – may I never forget!

7

If we were to live four ages, or even ten times four,
If we were known in the nine continents, and hailed as leader by all;
If we were to win good name, glory, and fame throughout the world,
But were denied the loving Gaze, we would be cast out,
Treated as the lowest of worms, accused as criminals.
Says Nanak, the bad are made virtuous and the virtuous granted
    more virtue,
But it is unthinkable that anyone could grant virtue to That One!

8

By hearing we become like the saints and gods,[20]
By hearing we fathom the earth, underworld, and skies,
By hearing we know the nine continents, the many worlds, and
    underworlds,
By hearing we are freed from the clutches of death;
Says Nanak, the devout enjoy bliss forever,
Hearing banishes suffering and evil.

9

Hearing makes us like Shiva, Brahma, and Indra,
Hearing makes the impious praise.
Hearing reveals ways of meditation and mysteries of the body,
Hearing illumines all treatises and scriptures.
    Says Nanak, the devout enjoy bliss forever,
Hearing banishes suffering and evil.

10

Hearing leads to truth, contentment, and knowledge,
Hearing bathes us in the sixty-eight sacred spots,
Hearing wins scholarly repute,
Hearing inspires peaceful contemplation;
Says Nanak, the devout enjoy eternal bliss,
Hearing banishes all suffering and evil.

11

By hearing we plumb the depths of virtues,
By hearing we rise to the status of sages and kings,
By hearing the blind find their way,

By hearing the unfathomable is fathomed;
Says Nanak, the devout enjoy eternal bliss,
Hearing banishes all suffering and evil.

12

No words can tell the state of faith,
Attempts to explain are later regretted.
No paper, pen, or scribe can describe it,
Nor any philosophizing help to realize it;
So wondrous is the Immaculate Name,
It is known only by those who hold it in their mind.

13

Having faith our mind and intellect awaken,
Having faith we learn of all the worlds;
Having faith we are safe from blows and pain;
Having faith we part company with death.
So wondrous is the Immaculate Name,
It is known only by those who hold it in their mind.

14

Having faith we walk on a clear path;
Having faith we advance in honor and glory;
   Having faith we do not stray down lanes and byways;
Having faith we keep to righteousness.
So wondrous is the Immaculate Name,
It is known only by those who hold it in their mind.

15

Having faith we find the door to liberation
Having faith our family is liberated too
Having faith we swim and lead our companions to the shore
Having faith, says Nanak, we need not go round begging for freedom.
So wondrous is the Immaculate Name,
It is known only by those who hold it in their mind.

16

The chosen win approval, they are the chosen ones.
The chosen receive honors in the Court,

The chosen shine splendidly at the Royal Gate,
The chosen meditate on the one and only Guru.
If we speak or think of the Creator's deeds,
There can be no calculation.
The bull that bears the earth is righteousness, child of compassion,
Its rope is contentment, holding the earth in balance.
All who see, live the life of truth.
How heavy the weight borne by the bull!
For there is not one earth but many more above and beyond!
Who stands beneath supporting them all?
This diversity of creatures, classes, and colors
Has been written in a single stroke of the Pen.
Who knows to write this infinite Writ?
What an infinite Writ to write.
What power and beauty of form!
How to estimate the gift,
This expanse from a single command,
Millions of rivers flowing forth at once.
How can I express the Primal Power?
I cannot offer myself to you even once!
Only that which pleases you is good.
You are forever constant, Formless One!

17

Countless are the ways of meditation,
    and countless the avenues of love,
Countless the ways of worship,
    and countless the paths of austerity and sacrifice.
Countless the texts, and countless the reciters of Vedas[21]
Countless the yogis turning away from the world,
Countless the devout reflecting on virtue and knowledge,
Countless the pious, and countless the givers,
Countless the warriors with faces scarred by iron
Countless the sages sunk in silent trance.
How can I express the Primal Power?
Not even once can I offer myself to you!
Only that which pleases you is good.
You are forever constant, Formless One!

18

Countless the fools densely blind
Countless the thieves living off others
Countless the tyrants bullying their way
Countless the cut-throats savaging their prey
Countless the evil trailing misdeeds behind them
Countless the liars spinning in lies
Countless the perverts devouring filth
Countless the slanderers stooped beneath their burden.
After thinking, lowly Nanak says this
Not even once can I offer myself to you!
Only that which pleases you is good.
You are forever constant, Formless One!

19

Countless are your names and countless your places,
Unreachable and unfathomable are your countless spheres;
Declaring them "countless" we increase our burden.
Yet, by words we name, by words we acclaim,
By words we know, sing, and praise.
By words we speak, by words we write,
By words we communicate and unite.
By words all our actions are written,
But Who writes, is above all writing.
As it is spoken, so are all allotted.
Wide as creation expands the Name,
There is no place without the Name.
How can I express the Primal Power?
Not even once can I offer myself to you!
Only that which pleases you is good.
You are forever constant, Formless One!

20

Dirty hands, feet, and body
Are washed clean with water;
Urine-stained clothes
Are washed with soap as well.
The mind polluted by evil
Is cleansed by the brilliance of the Name.

Good and evil are not mere words,
For our actions are written and go with us,
We reap only what we sow,
Nanak says, by the Will, we come and go.

21

Any merit eked from pilgrimage, austerity, mercy and charity,
Is barely worth a sesame seed.
Hearing, remembering, and loving the Name,
Immerses us in the sacred font within.
Every virtue rests in you, I have none in me,
Without virtue, devotion is impossible.
Salutations! you are the world, the Word, the Creator,
You are Truth, you are Beauty, you are Joy Eternal.
What was the time, what was the hour,
What was the date, what was the day,
What was the season, what was the month,
When creation was born?
Had pundits the answer, it would be written in the Puranas
Had qadis the answer, it would be written in the Qur'an
No ascetic knows the date or day, no one knows the month or season.
The Creator Who designed this creation alone knows.
How can I speak of you? How can I praise you?
How can I describe you? How can I know you?
Nanak says, many speak of you, each outsmarting the other.
Great is the Sovereign; great is Its Name, all that happens is Its doing.
Says Nanak, but those who claim credit, stay unadorned in the hereafter.

22

Worlds below worlds, worlds above worlds!
Tired of seeking their limits, the Vedas say one thing,
Arabic texts speak of eighteen thousand worlds traced to one source.
If It could be written, It would be written, but the writing passes.
Nanak says, praise the Great Who knows Itself.

23

Extollers extol but cannot fathom you,
As streams and rivulets flow to the ocean, not knowing its expanse.

Kings and sultans may rule over kingdoms vast as oceans,
    possess wealth piled high as mountains,
Yet none can match an ant whose heart does not forget.

24

Infinite is your glory, and infinite the ways to sing your praise,
Infinite are the deeds, and infinite the gifts;
Infinite is the seeing, and infinite the hearing,
And infinite are the workings of That Mind;
Infinite is the variety of forms,
Infinite are the edges of the universe.
And how many yearn to comprehend the limits?
They number without limit.
The end eludes all:
The more it is expressed, the farther it extends.
The Sovereign is great and high in station,
Yet higher still is the Name.
If we could ever reach that height
Only then would we know the Highest of the high!
Expansive as It is, It alone can know Itself
Nanak says, we are blessed with the gift of the Gaze.

25

Favor abounds beyond all reckoning,
Great is the Giver, with no trace of greed.
How many great heroes beg from you
And how many more, we cannot know!
Many exhaust themselves in vicious deeds,
Many receive but deny their Giver,
Many fools eat and eat
Many endure pain, hunger, suffering
Yet these too are your gifts, Giver.
Your Will frees us from bondage
No one here can intercede,
The fool who dares speak
Alone knows the blows on his face
It Itself knows, It Itself gives;
But few acknowledge this;

The person gifted to praise and adore
Nanak says, is indeed monarch of monarchs.

26

Priceless are the virtues, priceless their trade,
Priceless are the dealers, priceless the treasures in store;
Priceless are they who come for this trade,
    priceless what they take away;
Priceless is love, priceless those immersed in it.
Priceless is the law, and priceless the court,
Priceless are the scales, priceless the weights.
Priceless is the bounty, priceless the seal,
Priceless is the favor, priceless the command.
How priceless the Priceless One is, no one can say
Those who try sink into a silent trance.
Vedas and Puranas have also sought to say,
Scholars say in their texts and discourses.
Brahmas say, Indras say,
Gopis and Krishnas say,
Shivas say, Siddhas say,
Innumerable Buddhas say,
The demons say, the gods say,
The virtuous, wise, and devout say.
How many speak and begin to speak
Many have spoken and gone
And if their numbers were doubled again
Still no one could say.
That One is as great as It chooses to be,
Nanak says, only the True One knows Itself.
That babbler who presumes to say
Is marked as the fool of fools.

27

What kind of a gate is it, what kind of a mansion
    where you sit and support your creation?
Countless are the instruments and melodies,
    countless the players singing your praise!
Countless are the musical measures and their harmonies,
    countless the singers!

Wind, water, and fire sing your praise!
At your doorstep Dharmaraja sings your praise!,
His attendants, Chitra and Gupta, recording every deed, sing your praise
    while Dharmaraja checks on their records.
Shiva, Brahma, and the Goddess sing your praise,
    radiant with your splendor!
Indra seated upon his throne, in a circle of gods, sings your praise![22]
Ascetics in their meditation and sages in contemplation, sing your praise!
Celibates, saints, and the serene sing your praise!
Invincible heroes sing your praise!
Scholars and great seers with their texts in every age, sing your praise!
Beautiful women, enchanting the mind in the celestial, terrestrial, and
    nether worlds, sing your praise!
Jewels that come from you, spots made sacred by you, sing your praise!
Heroes and mighty warriors sing your praise!
The four sources of life sing your praise!
The continents, constellations, and universes you uphold, sing your praise!
Those who win your affection sing your praise –
    your devotees revel in your love!
How many other singers and players, I cannot conceive!
        Says Nanak, how then can I think of them?
That One, ever true Sovereign, true is the praise of that True One.
That One is, ever will be, and never will that Creator of the world not be!
Designer of this colorful diversity
        Creator of this variegated world,
You watch over and sustain your creation.
    All praise belongs to you.
Whatever you desire comes to pass, none can challenge your commands.
    Nanak says, you are the Sovereign of sovereigns; all abide by your Will.

28

Wear contentment, not the earrings of a yogi,
    let honest actions be your pouch and begging bowl,
    make inner contemplation your penitential ashes.
Death shall be the cloak you wear,
    pure living, your yogic discipline,
    and faith the staff you lean upon.
Accept all humans as your equals, and let them be your only sect.
    Conquering ourselves, we conquer the world!

Salutations!
Salutations to That One Who is primal, immaculate, immortal, immutable,
    Ever constant through the ages!

29

With knowledge as the banquet, and compassion as the hostess,
    let the divine music resonate in every heart.
The One is supreme, the whole cosmos under Its sway,
    why revere feats and miracles which lead you astray?
Meeting and parting are the rhythm of the universe,
    to all is given what is written.
Salutations!
Salutations to That One Who is primal, immaculate, immortal, immutable,
    Ever constant through the ages!

30

Our mother, the visible world, ingeniously gave birth to three sons:
The creator, the sustainer, and the one who holds the court.
But everything goes as It decrees, and all are under Its command.
It watches over all, and, Marvel of marvels, remains invisible to all!
Salutations!
Salutations to That One Who is primal, immaculate, immortal, immutable,
    Ever constant through the ages!

31

Its dwelling is in every realm. So too Its treasures.
Whatever is there, was put once and forever.
After making, the Maker regards Its creation.
Nanak says, the works of the True One are true forever.
Salutations!
Salutations to That One Who is primal, immaculate, immortal, immutable,
    Ever constant through the ages!

32

If one tongue became a hundred thousand tongues,
    and each of these became twenty times more,
And all recited it a hundred thousand times,
    the Owner of the world has but one Name.
We climb the stairs to union with you

Hearing of those who reach those heights,
    even the lowest are stirred to imitate.
Nanak says, the Gaze is received, the boasting of the false is false.

33

It is not ours to speak or stay silent
It is not ours to ask or give
It is not ours to live or die
It is not ours to gain riches that rattle the mind
It is not ours to have consciousness, knowledge, and reflection,
It is not ours to be liberated from the cycle of life and death.
The One, Whose power it is, regards Its doing.
Nanak says, no one is high or low.

34

Amid nights and seasons, dates and days,
Amid air, water, fire, and netherworlds,
The earth is placed, the place for righteous action.
In it are colorful beings and lifestyles
Infinite are their names and infinite their forms.
We are judged on every action performed;
The One is True and Its verdicts are truly just.
Those accepted become radiant,
They glow with the mark of the Gaze;
The raw and the ripened,[23]
Nanak says, reaching there, become known.

35

Such is the order of the realm of Duty,
Now tell us about the realm of Knowledge.
How many airs, waters, and fires!
    How many Krishnas and Shivas!
How many Brahmas, and in what variety of forms, colors,
    and guises they are created!
How many earths and mountains to live and act on,
    how many saints, like Dhru, and their sermons!
How many Indras, moons, and suns, how many continents and universes!
How many ascetics, enlightened ones, and yogic masters,
    how many goddesses!

How many gods, demons, and sages, how many jewels and oceans!
How many species, how many languages, and how many rulers and kings!
How many revelations, how many devotees!
    Says Nanak, there is no end to their end!

36

In the Realm of Knowledge, knowledge blazes forth,
Here reign mystic melodies and myriad sports and joys.
Now the Realm of Beauty is beauty itself:
Here the faculties are honed in unmatched splendor;
Words fail to describe,
They who try regret their lack.
Here consciousness, wisdom, mind, and discernment are sharpened,
Awareness sharpened like that of the gods and mystics.

37

The Realm of Action is full of force:
Here is the One, with no other.
Here heroes and mighty warriors dwell
Inspired by Ram
Here are Sita and women of her fame and virtue,
Their beauty beyond words;
They do not die, they are not beguiled,
For Ram is in their hearts;
Saints from many worlds live in this Realm of Action:
    They know bliss, for the True One is imprinted on their minds.
In the Realm of Truth, the Formless One is at home
Gazing upon Its creation.
Here are continents, constellations, and universes,
Whose limits cannot be told
Here are people of various forms –
All acting according to the Will.
It watches, rejoices, and contemplates Its own creation,
Nanak says, to describe this is as hard as iron.

38

Let continence be your smithy, and patience your goldsmith;
Let wisdom be your anvil, and knowledge your hammer;
Let awe be the bellows, and inner control the blazing fire;

In the crucible of love, let the ambrosia flow;
In this true mint, forge the Word.
Such fulfillment comes to those blessed with the Gaze;
Says Nanak, happy are they who are gazed upon.

Epilogue

Air is our Guru, water our father,
     the great earth is our mother;
Day and night are the female and male nurses –
     the whole universe plays in their laps.
Good and bad deeds are disclosed before the Law,
     Our actions take us near or far.
Those who remember the Name,
     they earn true success;
Nanak says their faces shine,
     they liberate many along with themselves.

Arati

The sky is our platter; the sun and moon, lamps,
    it is studded with pearls, the starry galaxies,
The wafting scent of sandalwood is the incense,
    the gentle breeze, our fly whisk,
    all vegetation, the bouquet of flowers we offer to you.

What a worship!
This truly is your worship, you who sunder life from death.
The unstruck sound within is the drum to which we chant.

You have a thousand eyes yet without an eye you are,
You have a thousand faces yet without a face you are,
You have a thousand feet yet without a foot you are,
You have a thousand noses yet without a nose you are.
    I am enchanted by your wonders!

There is a light in all, and that light is you;
By your light we are all lit.
Light sparkles from knowledge,
Whatever pleases you is your worship!

My mind is greedy as a bumblebee,
Day and night I long to drink
    the ambrosia of your lotus-feet
Nanak says, grant nectar to this thirsty bird –
    Grant me a dwelling in your Name.

(GG: 663)

The Fish and the Ruby

You are the enjoyer, you are the joy,
    You are the ravisher too;
You are the bride in her dress,
    You are the spouse on the nuptial bed.
My beloved is dyed in love –
Fully permeating everyone!

You are the fisherman, you are the fish,
    You are the waters, you are the trap;
You are the weight that holds the net,
You are the lost ruby swallowed by the fish.

My love is imbued
In a myriad colors, my friends.
The virtuous bride perpetually enjoys her spouse,
      But here am I sitting all alone!

Says Nanak, this is my plea: join me with you!
    You are the pool, you are the swan,
You are the lotus in the day,
You are the lily of the night,
    You watch them, you rejoice!

                                              (GG: 23)

Be Like the Bride

If we forget our beloved for an instant,
    We suffer terribly.
If you are not lodged in our minds,
    How will we be honored at your door?
By meeting the Guru, we find peace,
    By divine praise, devouring fires burn out.

O my mind, remember divine virtues day and night.
Those who never forget you
    Are rare in this world!

With our light merged in yours –
    Our consciousness tuned in with yours,
Violence and selfishness slip away;
    There is no more doubt or sorrow.
Those whose hearts hold the One,
    The Guru leads them to their divine union.

If we make our body like that of a bride,
    The Enjoyer will take pleasure in us;
Do not fall in love with anything
    That is fleeting.
The virtuous are like an auspicious wife:
    She enjoys the divine spouse on her bed.

The four fires are extinguished
    By the waters from the divine font;
A lotus blooms wide inside,
    Thirst is quenched by an ambrosial flow.
Says Nanak, befriend the Guru,
    So you will receive truth at the divine door.

(GG: 21–22)

Guru Arjan

ಖಾ ಔ

Neither Hindu nor Muslim

I do not keep fasts
  Nor Ramadan.
I serve the One
  Who defends till the end.
I have One Gosain,
  I have One Allah.
Hindus and Muslim
  Both receive justice from this One.
I do not go on Hajj to the Ka'ba
  I do not go for Puja on Tiratha(s)
I serve the One
  And no other.
I do not perform Puja
  I do not recite the Namaz
I have taken up the formless One –
  Whom I exalt in my heart.
I am not Hindu
  I am not Muslim,
I am the body and breath
  Of Allah and Ram.
As Kabir has said,
Meeting Guru or Pir
  I discover my Husband myself.

(GG: 1136)

Font of Joy

You are our sovereign,
    To you we pray:
Our body and life
    Are your gifts.
You are our mother,
    You are our father,
    We are your children;
You are the font of countless joys.

No one knows your extent:
You are higher than the highest!
Our whole cosmos is beaded
    On your thread,
All that happens is by your will.

Your reality and parameters,
    You alone know,
Says Nanak the slave,
    I offer myself to you!

(GG: 268)

Epilogue (to the Guru Granth)

On the platter, three things lie:
    Truth, Contentment, Reflection;
They contain the ambrosial Name,
    By which we are sustained.
They who eat, they who savor,
    They are liberated.
This thing must not be abandoned,
    Ever and ever, keep it in your heart.
The dark ocean can be crossed,
    If we take hold of the Guru's feet.
Says Nanak, all existence is the Divine's expanse.

Sheikh Farid

ॐ ॐ

Blessed Are the Mothers

Those who nurture love in their hearts
    They alone are true;
But whose lips say things other than their hearts
Know them as false.
Those who nurture love for Khuda,
    They are ecstatic for divine vision;
But who forget the Name,
    They are mere burden on earth.
The Divine fastens real dervishes –
    To the hem of its own robes,
Blessed are the mothers,
    Who give birth to such devotees!
    Blessed is their coming into the world.
O sustainer –
    You are limitless, unfathomable, infinite!
Those who discern your truth,
    Let me kiss their feet!
I seek your protection, O'Khuda,
    You are our great giver;
Sheikh Farid asks your blessing:
    Let me serve you forever.

(GG: 488)

Fasten Yourself to Allah

Says Sheikh Farid, my dear friend,
    Fasten yourself to Allah;
Soon this body will turn to dust,
    And land in its paltry home, the grave.
You could meet Allah today, Sheikh Farid
    If you calm your crane-like flapping mind!
If only I knew
    There'd be no return to life,
I'd not have clung to illusions
    And ruined myself.
Religion demands we speak truth;
    Not deception
Disciples must walk the path
    Shown by their teacher.
Seeing the handsome youths go across
    The fair woman is inspired.
But those who seek glittering gold,
    Are sawn in two.
O Sheikh in this fleeting world,
    Nothing remains still;
This place where we now sit
    How many have sat and gone!
Cranes appear in the fall,
    Forest fires in summer,
Lightning in monsoon,
In winter, the wife embraces her husband
And adorns his form.
So, all is motion and flux
    Remember our transient life;
It takes months for the body to form,
    Alas, a mere instant to go.
O Farid, the earth asks the sky,
    "How many boatmen have gone by?"
"Some were cremated in fire, some lie in graves;
    They bear the result of their actions."

(GG: 488)

Dried Up Breasts

When it was time to make a raft
You did not make yourself one;
Now that the waves leap high
How difficult it is to stay afloat!

Why hold the saffron flower?
Its color runs, my dear.

You are weak to begin with, and
The husband's order is strong;
Your breasts cannot flow
With milk any more.

Says Farid, O dear friends
    When our husband calls,
The swan of duality will fly away
    Our body will be a heap of dust.

(GG: 794)

Says Farid (selected couplets)

Says Farid, I saw the tender eyes
That enticed the world –
They couldn't endure an eyeliner
    Today birds hatch their young in them! (14)

Brown sugar, white sugar, rock candy,
    Molasses, honey, rich buffalo milk
– All these are delicious things, but
    O Rabb, none come close to you! (27)

Bathed and washed and dressed up,
    She comes and sleeps in oblivion;
Says Farid she loses the fragrance of musk;
    She stinks like *hingu* [asafetida]. (33)

Anxiety is my cot, misery its strings;
    Pangs of separation are my sheets and blanket.
Says Farid, O my true husband, behold:
    This is my life. (35)

Such painful pangs of separation!
    Indeed, your longing rules us all;
The body that does not long for the lover,
    Says Farid, know it as a burial ground. (36)

These sprouts around are poisonous –
    They are coated in sugary paste;
Says Farid, some died while they sowed them,
    Others when they harvested. (37)

The day is lost loafing around,
    Night is lost in sleep;
When asked for the writ:
    Is this all you did? (38)

Sheikh Farid has grown old,
    His body tremors;
Even if we were to live a hundred years,
    This body will turn to dust. (41)

Some have extra flour
    Some not even a pinch of salt;
Says Farid, let them go ahead and see
    Who fares worse. (44)

All those who were honored with recitations and bugles,
– Welcomed with the beat of drums
    With canopies over their heads, says Farid,
Today they lie asleep in desolate grounds,
    – Buried like destitute orphans. (45)

Even as the two lamps shine,
        The angel of death sneaks in;
He seizes the fortress, he plunders the heart,
        He extinguishes the lamps on his way out. (48)

Look what happens to the cotton
To the sesame seed, to the sugarcane
        to the paper, to the pot and the coals –
Says Farid, this would be their punishment
        Who do evil deeds. (49)

You don a prayer-mat on your shoulders,
        A Sufi shawl around your neck;
Your words are sweet as molasses,
        But your heart is like a knife;
Your face is so bright, says Farid,
        Your mind is pitch-black. (50)

Not a drop of blood would spill
        If my body were cut; says Farid,
Those who are imbued in love for Rabb,
        Their bodies are devoid of blood. (51)

Says Farid, the beautiful vessel shatters
        Its lovely thread is snapped;
Azrail, the messenger of death,
        Whose house is he visiting today? (68)

Every heart is a jewel,
        Make sure you don't break any;
If you desire your beloved;
        Do not hurt anyone! (130)

Bhagat Namdev

ॐ ॐ

The Power of Love

Laughing and playing
    I entered your door
While worshipping,
I Namdev, was grabbed
    And driven out.

My caste is terribly low,
    O king of Yadavs!
Why was I born into
    A family of calico printers?

I picked up my blanket
    And started to walk,
I went out and sat way
    Behind the temple wall.

Just as I Namdev
    Began to praise your name,
The temple turned around
    To face your devoted slave.

(GG: 1164)

Precious Name

We may practice asceticism in Benares,
We may die at a pilgrim spot standing on our head,
Our body may be burnt in fire,
We may even find a way for our body to live forever,
We may perform the horse sacrifice,
We may secretly make offerings of gold,
– But nothing equals the worship of Ram's Name!

(GG: 973)

This Is That

A white lotus bloomed in the forest
The swans and beings came from its petals
Behold: the dance of creation dancing in Krishna!

First was Purusha
From Purusha came Maya
All this is That.
In this garden we all dance
Like water in brimming well-pots.

Women and men dance
They are no other than the Dancer.
Don't doubt
Don't fear
Says Krishna, "See! This all is me."

Like the pots on the Persian wheel
The world goes round and round
Wandering and lost, I have come to your door
Who are you?
It's me.
Namdev.
Please save me
From this world
and from Yama, the lord of death!

(GG: 694)

I Come to You

O my father, O wealthy Madho,
My longhaired dark lover!
You descended from paradise with disc in hand
    To save the life of the helpless elephant!
In the court of Duhshasana you clothed Draupadi
    Like cirles swirling in the sky!
You rescued Ahalya, Gautam's wife,
      How many more have you freed?
A lowly outcaste Namdev,
      Comes to you for refuge!

                                    (GG: 988)

Blessed Is the Wool

Blessed blessed
Is the flute of Ram
For melodious
Is its unstruck melody
Blessed Blessed
Is the wool of sheep
And blessed is its shawl   .
Worn by Krishna.

Blessed Blessed
Are you mother Devaki
In your home was born
Kamala's handsome husband
Blessed Blessed
Are the forests of Brindaban
Where dallies Lord Narayan!

He plays the flute,
    He grazes the cows
Namdev's Master
Sports ever in bliss.

                                    (GG: 988)

Every Heart Beats with Ram

In every heart speaks Ram,
    Yes, Ram speaks;
Who would speak
      Other than Ram?
Of the same clay is the elephant, the ant,
      And so many other forms and shapes;
Standing still or moving, worms or moths,
      Every heart beats with Ram.
Have but one concern:
      Keep infinite Ram
Give up all else!
Says Nama:
      I have no desire!
Who is the master?
      Who is the slave?

(GG: 988)

Bhagat Ravidas

ಕ ಿ

What's the Difference?

Between you and me
    And me and you
What difference
    Can there be?
Like the gold and its bracelet?
    The water and its wave?
If I did no wrong, O infinite One,
    Would you be called a redeemer?
You are the Master,
    You are the knower of hearts;
You are known because of your devotee,
    And your devotee, because of you!
Give me knowledge
    So I may worship you;
Says Ravidas, rare is the person who sees
    That One exists equally in every heart.

(GG: 93)

Free in the Knot

If you are the mountain,
I am the peacock;
If you are moon,
I am the *chakora* bird in love.

O my love, don't leave me,
I won't leave you;
If I break off with you,
Who would I go to?

If you are the lamp,
I am the wick;
If you are the sacred spot,
I am the pilgrim.

In my true love,
I am bound with you;
Tied to you,
I am free of all others!

(GG: 658)

All the Pure Is Impure

The suckling calf
Polluted the milk,
Bees polluted the flower,
    And the fish the water.

O mother mine,
    What do I offer the Divine?
There are no flowers worthy of worship
    All the pure we know is impure.

Snakes are coiled around
    The sandalwood tree:
Poison and ambrosia,
So close together!

There is no incense or lamp
No food or flower
That is pure enough
For your worship.

Our body and mind
    We must dedicate to you
With the Guru's gift
    We can attain the absolute Pure.

Since I can't make ritual sacrifices
    Nor offer any flowers
Says Ravidas,
    I wonder how I'll fare!

(GG: 525)

Oblivion

When I exist,
You do not;
Now that you exist,
I do not.
The waves
Surge
They merge –
Water with water.
O beloved, what a mirage!
Reality is not what we image.

A king is asleep
On his throne;
He dreams
He is a beggar!
He has it all,
Yet suffers in oblivion.
Such is our condition.

(GG: 657)

Your Name Is My Worship

Your Name is my worship
   Your Name is my sacred bath
Except the divine Name
   Everything is false.

Your Name is my prayer mat,
   Your Name is the mortar [to make sandalpaste]
Your Name is the saffron
   I sprinkle You with.

Your Name is the water
   Your Name is sandalwood –
Grinding it into paste is reciting Your Name
   All that is Yours is offered to You!

Your Name is the lamp
   Your Name is the wick
Your Name is the oil
   I pour into it.

Your Name is the flame
That lights up all the worlds.

Your Name is the thread
   Your Name is the garland of flowers,
All other vegetation
   Is too tainted for You.

Everything belongs to You –
   So what offering can I make?
Your own Name is the fan
   I wave over you.
The world is lost in ritual and scriptures,
   To sixty-eight pilgrim spots, to the four classes.
My Arati, says Ravidas, is solely Your Name
   Your true Name is the food I offer to You!

                                 (GG: 694)

Meet Me Quickly

My lowly circle
    I think of day and night;
My actions are shameful,
    My birth, despicable.

O Ram, O Gusain,
    You are the life of all lives,
Don't forget me:
    I am yours.

Take away my suffering
    Grant me your blessing;
I won't leave your feet, though
    My body could go.

Says Ravidas:
    I seek your shelter;
Meet me quickly
    Do not delay!

                                               (GG: 345)

Wake Up

The day that comes
     That day must go
Whatever we do
     Won't be forever.

Our friends departed,
     So must we;
Long may be the path
     But death hovers above.

This life, this world
     You took to be true?
Why are you asleep my mind?
     Wake up from your oblivion!

The One who gave you life
     Will also feed and clothe,
That One runs its shop
     In your each and every pore.

Fill yourself with devotion
     Rid yourself of me and mine
At this morning hour
     Hold the Name in your heart.

Life is going by
     You haven't paved your road
Soon it will be evening
     And darkness will take over.

Says Ravidas,
O ignorant fool
Don't you know,
     This world is a funeral home?

(GG: 793)

2

BELOVED SUFI POETS

Throughout Muslim rule in the Punjab, Arabic and Persian were vitally important languages. Arabic was the language of the holy Qur'an and of theology, while Persian was the language of administration and that of "elite" Sufism. But Bullhe Shah and Waris Shah (and many other prominent Muslims; see the introduction) produced poetry in the local Punjabi and were immediately imprinted on the lips and hearts of the people. Though popular stories about their lives are still a living force in all segments of society, there is very little historical documentation on either of them. Scholars generally accept that Bullhe Shah was born in a village near Kasur (now in Pakistan) in 1680 in a Sayyid family (the Prophet Muhammad was a Sayyid) during the reign of the last powerful Mughal emperor, Aurangzeb. His father, a migrant from Baghdad, taught in a mosque. Bullhe Shah had two sisters, and none of the siblings ever married. He became the disciple of Inayat Shah (d. 1735), a member of the Qadiri order of Sufism. But since Bullhe did not fully follow the Islamic codes, his Master ended up rejecting him. On his own then he went about singing and dancing and composing poetry, and after 12 years when Inayat Shah heard him sing, he accepted Bullhe Shah back.[1] From Bullhe's verse we learn that his Master belonged to the low gardener class of Arains, which created much tension in his family and community. About Waris Shah we know even less. From his writing, scholars assess that he was born somewhere around 1735 (a few decades after Bullhe Shah), in the village of Sheikhupura (which is now a part of Pakistan as well), that he belonged to an elite Sayyid family (like Bullhe Shah), and studied with a Sufi Pir from the city of Kasur (close to Bullhe Shah's birthplace). It is believed that he was orphaned early in life.[2] Legend has it that he fell in love with a woman named Bhagbhari, and having been driven away from her village, he started to compose Heer's romance – with a broken heart.[3]

Overall we are left with a picture of two poets from about the same age, the same region, and the same social status. Their north Indian landscape rich with Sufi, Islamic, Sikh, and Bhakti Hindu currents was abuzz with a range of romances, equivalent of Juliet and Romeo to reuse the analogy. While some like Heer-Ranjha, Sassi-Punnu, and Sohni-Mahival were indigenous to the Punjab, others like Shirin-Farhad were Persian in origin and even Arabic like Zulaikha-Yusuf. In this culturally fluid space, Bullhe Shah and Waris Shah challenged the rigid norms of their times; through the motif of romantic love, they tried to spread the message of religious tolerance and harmony. In their deceptively simple idioms and metaphors of Punjabi countryside we discover highly sophisticated Sufi ideals of *wahdat al-wujud* (unicity of Being), *fana* (annihilation of the individual ego), and *baqa* (subsistence in the Divine); complex human emotions of love, hate, jealousy; and experiences religious and erotic. Indeed Bullhe Shah and Waris Shah are beloved by Punjabis of all faiths, and are even appropriated by these faiths as their own. Their mausoleums have become important sites of pilgrimage, and their poetry is an essential part of the folk culture of both sides of the Punjab. It has been recited at weddings and social events for generations. In contemporary Indian pop music, songwriters use their lyrics. Many are being adapted into romantic Bollywood songs. Bullhe Shah's highly metaphysical poem "Bullah Wonders Who He Is" (*Bulla Ki Jana Main Kaun*) was played by Junoon, the modern Sufi rock band from Pakistan. It was also made into a Rock/Fusion song by Rabbi Shergill. From amateur singers to internationally acclaimed artists, Muslims, Hindus, and Sikhs alike sing the "portable" Bullhe Shah's songs.[4] Indeed, the ecumenical pulsations of the Sufi poets have acquired a new poignancy of cultural unity lost to the Punjabis on both sides of the Border.

My selections from Bullhe Shah come from his famous *Kafian* (short lyric stanzas interspersed by a refrain), which continue to be sung in formal sessions of Sufi singing (*qawalli*).[5] Numerous collections of verses attributed to Bullhe Shah in Indo-Persian and Gurmukhi scripts first appear in late nineteenth century. As Robin Rinehart alerts us, these collections were transcribed from poems of his that were sung at qawalli sessions, and so they include alterations and interpolations by the singers. There is no reliable text of his poetry; instead, there is "only a Bullhe Shah tradition, a body of poetry attributed to Bullhe Shah."[6] There is a similar problem with Waris Shah, since there is a gap of several decades between the time his text was composed (1766) and the earliest manuscript to date (1821). According to Jeevan Deol, a specialist in Punjabi manuscripts, the other extant manuscripts are longer, and the numerous printed editions use these long manuscripts, which also interpolate verses from famous poets.[7] Though their verses have come down to us in a "notoriously corrupt"[8] manuscript tradition, they still play powerfully on the emotions and intellect, and serve as an important moral guide.

Very much in the manner of the Guru Granth poets, Bullhe Shah and Waris Shah condemn ritualistic hypocrisy and stress interior devotion. They boldly speak against religious conflicts:

> *Hindu na nahin Musalman*
> *Bahie trinjan taj abhiman*
> *Sunni na nahin ham Shia*
> *Sulha kul ka marag lia*

> We are not Hindu, we are not Muslim,
> So let us give up our pride, and do our spinning;
> We are neither Sunni nor Shia;
> We are a family, so let us live in harmony.

> ("Neither Sinners nor Saints")

Bullhe Shah's insights in the above passage reveal the root of our global tragedies: the recent bomb blasts in mosques and temples and five star hotels in India or Pakistan, or the violent Sunni-Shia struggle going on in Iraq (and spreading in Arab and Persian nations) arise from artificial notions of inflated egotism. Narcissistic obsessions shut out genuine love for the Divine, the absolute singular One – common to each and all. "Such is my enlightenment: Hindu or Muslim is irrelevant," declares Bullhe Shah loud and clear. As he goes on to say in his poem entitled "There is a Thief in my Shawl," Hindus cremate their dead and Muslims bury their dead, but they needlessly scorn the *other*'s way. Due to external factors like geography and climate, communities may develop different patterns and customs, but they are the same at the basic human level. The poet categorically says that there is nothing essential that divides Hindu from Muslim, or Sunni from Shia; it is merely artificial pride that gets densely congealed and obstructs people from recognizing their unity.

In a cotton-growing region, the ubiquitous household chore of spinning naturally becomes significant; for the Sufi, Sikh, and Hindu poets alike, its syncopated rhythm symbolizes divine contemplation. The movement of the stars and planets, the whirl of electrons and protons, the ebb and tide of life, the flow of the infinite into the finite – are choreographed in spinning cotton into thread at the spinning wheel. The mesmerizing circularity dissolves the selfish ego, opening conduits of freedom, gratitude, and love. The poet's call to sit and spin together (*bahie trinjan*) is extremely relevant in today's mechanically operated and fundamentally disjointed society.

More specifically, "spinning" symbolizes *dhikr*, the entrancing Sufi spiritual exercises intended to bring one closer to God. This typical female activity of spinning parallels other domestic activities such as grinding grain and rocking babies. Historian Richard Eaton contributes the spread of Sufism in the Deccan to the link between bodily movements and rhythmic recitations by women engaged in their daily chores. As he explains, devotional Sufi phrases were interjected into the vernacular Deccani folk songs – *charkhi-namas*, *chakki-namas*, and *lori-namas*. As women sang while spinning on their *charkhas*, grinding grain on their *chhakis*, and rocking their babies with *loris* (lullabies), the mystical recitations were absorbed in their cyclical motions.[9] Punjabi folk songs naturally saturated with Sufi ideas have exerted a similar influence on the local population. While performing ordinary household chores, essential Islamic ideals in their simplest form were internalized by the rural Punjabis. The Sufi theme of circularity is visible in Punjabi dancers and drummers as they spin performing *bhangra* (traditional male folkdance) and *gidda* (female folkdance) to mesmerizing folk songs imbued with Sufi lore.

Following the tradition of mainstream Sufism, Bullhe Shah and Waris Shah posit passionate love as the highest form of religious experience, and so they simultaneously spin the erotic and divine fibers into their literary texture. Physical love (*ishq-e majazi*) is essential for metaphysical love (*ishq-e haqiqi*), a material thread that binds humans with the Divine: "can a needle sew without thread?" poses Bullhe Shah acutely. They denounce religious orthodoxy; they reject formalism and ceremonies, and even substitute the essential pillars of Islam with the rapture of love. "Why must I turn towards the Ka'ba, when my lover lives in Takht Hazara?" asks Bullhe Shah. His lover's village stands in for the Ka'ba, the prototypical Islamic shrine, and a visit there possesses the religious efficacy of pilgrimage to Mecca. The Sufi poet rejects the cultural ethos cultivated by many Mecca-

oriented Muslim theologians, scholars, and saints living on the
Subcontinent; their "extra-territorial cultural ethos" is shifted to the local
Punjabi territory.[10] Paradise is not a promise after death either; paradise is
right here, in the lover Ranjha's natal village. Institutional religion with all
its formalities and modes of worship is made redundant: "Those who
drink from the cup of love, why should they care about fasts or prayers?"
("Show Me the Way"). Addressing his psyche as a maternal subject:

> *roze hajj namaz ni mae*
> *mainun pia ne aan bhulae*

> Fasts, pilgrimage, and prayers, O'mother,
> My beloved came and made me forget!

("All Forgotten")

With a flash of the lover, the individual is freed from societal and religious
obligations. Liberation and ecstasy, the ideal experience for the Guru
Granth poets, is replayed by the Punjabi Sufi poets. Of course being rapt
in love is not a fool's paradise; paradoxically, the oblivion to traditional
rites and rituals produces for the poets an excruciating experience –
analogous to being "fried," "grinded," "burnt," "pierced." These images
denote the existential pain at the heart of the Sufi goal of annihilation
(*fana*).

And those who impose restrictions on the flow of love are vehemently
criticized. These include religious officials, community members, and the
immediate family. For instance, Waris Shah's protagonist Ranjha cheekily
confronts the Mullah and chastises him for his self-righteousness and
hypocrisy:

> With the beard of a Sheikh,
> The deeds of Satan,
> You ensnare passers by;
> With the Qur'an in hand,
> Perched on the *minbar*,
> You cast the nets of deceit...

(*Heer Waris Shah*, p. 40)

Not only the Mullahs – caretakers of mosques and leaders in prayers, but
also the Qazis – public officials who propagate the legalities of Islam,

emerge as reprehensible figures in Waris Shah's text. After all, only a lover can know the *sharia,* the divine law! The clergy with their institutions miss out on the inner vibrations of the heart and merely stress the exoteric codes of behavior. The Qazi who forces Heer to smother her love for Ranjha threatens her with violent consequences sanctioned by religious law: "the moment I declare the *fatwa*, you will be killed" (*Heer Waris Shah,* p. 74). That she will be flayed, that she will be thrown into blazing fire, that her tongue will be ripped out, are some of the other threats inflicted on the heroine in love. By capturing the brutal details of the punishments and the acid tone in which they were ordained, our pre-modern poets elicited a *responsible response* from their audience. These threats against Heer are eerily familiar and continue to elicit such a response in our own "modern" world as more and more women suffer under patriarchal codes of morality and honor.

While denouncing orthodox doctrines and their legal guardians, Bullhe Shah and Waris Shah underscore motifs from the intricate local Punjabi matrix in which religious boundaries were blurred. Again, in the context of our own insular twenty-first century, these Punjabi Sufi poets offer something quite remarkable. Both Bullhe Shah and Waris Shah clearly belong to the aniconic tradition of Islam, yet they sumptuously utilize Hindu imagery. But instead of appreciating the novel mutlivalency of their poetics, scholars frequently try to find chain-link patterns of historical influence and dependency. Regarding Bullhe Shah, Rinehart discusses the claims made by respective scholars that he is either a "Vedantic Sufi," "Vaisnava Vedantic Sufi," or a "strictly orthodox Muslim," and concludes that the authors appropriate him for their own agendas, give little attention to the actual content of his compositions, even misinterpret him, and end up providing "more about their own religious preferences than those of Bullhe Shah's."[11] The application of the genetic thrust to label the poets in either or categories blocks the dazzling diversity of the human spirit. There is no doubt that they participated in an intellectually vibrant milieu; in fact their vocabulary and imagery attests to their exposure to an environment charged with a spiritual dynamic and diversity. Without being chauvinistic or afraid of the "other," they reveal the pluralistic patterns of the human imagination. For instance, in "Krishna Plays the Magic Flute," Bullhe Shah concretely visualizes the handsome cowherd and acutely hears his mesmerizing melodies. As the poem progresses, the popular Hindu figure is spliced with his Muslim Prophet (Hazrat), just as the sound of Krishna's flute is fused in with the language of Islamic prayer

(Kalma). In fact, the attributes (*sifat*) of the magical flute flow from Being Itself (*wujud*); its singular note (*ikk sur*) breathes life (*dam mare*) into each and all (*sabh de vic*). The Sufi metaphysical subtext emerges explicitly in the final stanza of the poem:

> *Bullah puj pae takrar*
> > *buhe aan khalote yar*
> *Rakhin kalme nal biopar,*
> > *teri hazrat bhare gavahi*
> *Bansi kahan acaraj bajai*

> Says Bullhe: end all this conflict
> > Welcome friends to the door
> Do keep your deal with the Kalma,
> > So the Prophet (*hazrat*) will stand as your witness.
> *Krishna plays the magic flute*

Such magical confluences of the West Asian and Indian worlds filter throughout Punjabi Sufi poetry and give an exciting new impetus to conventional tropes and future relationships. Denis Matringe explores many interesting Hindu elements in Bullhe Shah's mystical message,[12] but again, if we look closely, each instance embraces multiple cultural allusions that defy any one religious label. For instance, the thief hiding in Bullhe's shawl (in "Bullah Wonders Who He Is") could be the naughty Krishna playing hide and seek with his beautiful maidens, just as it could be the majestic Hidden Treasure from the author's West Asian Sufi inheritance. As we know from a popular Islamic tradition, God speaks in the first person through the voice of the Prophet to explain the purpose of creation: "I was a Hidden Treasure. I loved to be known. Therefore I created the creation."[13]

Likewise, in Bullhe Shah's references to dance (for example in "Out of Tune, Out of Step"), readers can discover their own and different meaning:

> In whom dwells the Divine,
> They jump up calling,
> > "Beloved! O' Beloved!"

> They do not care for rules
>> They do not care for tunes,
> They play their own sports.
>> Those touched by perfect love,
> They dance out of tune
>> They dance out of step.

For those tuned into the popular Vaishnava devotional dances of *raslila* on the north Indian stage, Lord Krishna may quickly flash; for Shaivites, the image of Shiva Nataraja all whirl and twirl dancing in the circle of flames, may appear. But the movement of freedom and rapture could as easily belong to the Sufi *dhikr* practiced by the Whirling Dervishes or the "unveiled dancer" in Guru Nanak's poetry.[14] Christians could even read in it the primal paradox expressed by T.S. Eliot, "at the still point that is where the dance is" (*Four Quartets*). With Bullhe Shah, the primordial form of religiosity acquires a strong nonconformist message: the choreography of dance lies not in following external rules and patterns that confine movement, but in the "physical touch" (*tan lagia*) of "perfect love" (*ishq kamal*) which tears apart all fetters. While pointing out the absolute unicity of the Divine, the multiple cultural references fusing organically in Punjabi Sufi lyrics show the amazing breadth of the human imagination.

Indeed our poets open us to "an enchanted universe." In his classic text, Harjot Oberoi describes Muslims, Hindus, and Sikhs in pre colonial rural Punjab sharing with one another saints and sacred sites, stories and superstitions, spirits and exorcisms.[15] Antithetical to the officials of Islamic law and theology, Waris Shah depicts the benevolent five Pirs (saints), collectively owned by the Punjabis. There are some excellent studies on the practices venerating such figures[16] (perfectly translated as "fairy godmothers" by Chris Shackle[17]), and on their importance for the understanding of Punjab's cultural and religious history.[18] However, the seductive force of the Pirs for a Punjabi comes out most tellingly in Waris Shah's narrative itself. The five Pirs in his text exalt the universal emotion of love (*ishq*). Instead of admonishing the couple for bringing shame to their families, they instruct Heer and Ranjha to honor their love together: "*tusan dohan ne rabb nun yad karna, nahin ishq nun leek lagavanaee* – now you both must remember the divine; never must you put a blemish on love" ("To Ranjha and Heer: Blessings from the Five Pirs"). Their act of love entails remembering God together. Love is therefore the energy, which unites not only humans with the Divine, but also Heer with Ranjha –

female with male, a woman of high status with a buffalo-herd working for her father, and by implication, Muslim, Hindu, and Sikh. Their instruction highlights love (*ishq*) as the supreme principle. Truth and beauty itself, love must be attended to with utmost responsibility. And it demands courage. Anything that would blemish it (literally, "draw a line" *leek*/line, *lagavanee*/draw) – be it personal fears or religious restrictions or societal codes – has to be defied. The Pirs then bless Heer and Ranjha with the choicest Punjabi food consisting of *churi* (wheat bread crumbled with molasses and butter) and milk from the prized breed of the brown buffalo (*majj buri*)! In their advice and blessings the Pirs project the perfect Punjabi life, one in which divine love is fused in with secular affairs, religious devotion transcends sectarian divisions, and eating and drinking are conjoined with spirituality.

Experimenting with the occult was also common in rural Punjab. Some North Indian folk practices, like burning dried *harmal* seeds to ward off evil spirits, go back to pre-Islamic Zoroastrian Persia. Bullhe Shah fuels his literary discourse with just such an exorcism rite:

> In the furnace of my love,
>   I'll exorcise evil spirits:
> I'll toss in the stars
>   Like *harmal* seeds,
>   And burn them up
>   Like the heat of the sun.
> *With magic and spells,*
>   *I'll win my beloved.*
>
> ("Love Spells")

In a female voice the poet unwaveringly declares the tremendous power of the human spirit. The "furnace" of love is so intense and vast that the distant stars can be tossed in it; the emotion of love is so powerful that it can burn every obstacle.

It is not surprising that the *qissa* of "immortal romance" of Heer and Ranjha begins with a paean on love. The *qissa* is a narrative lyric, which combines Perso-Islamic and regional aesthetic forms, and typically begins with an invocation (*hamad*). Flowing out from Allah, Waris Shah glorifies love as the ontological "root of the universe" – "*jagu da mool.*" The birth of the cosmos, its reality, its space and time, and its entire functioning are therefore contingent on its force. Waris Shah invokes his divine subject while repeatedly drawing in his audience (four times he uses the term *mian*, a title of respect that connotes intimacy; translated below as "O'friend"). His story is prefaced with the reminder that the archetypal lover is Allah; the primordial beloved, the Prophet Muhammad:

> *Aval hamad khuda da virad kije*
> *Ishq kita su jag da mool mian*
> *Pahilan aap Allah ne ishq kita*
> *Te mashuk hai nabi rasul mian*
> *Ishq pir faqir da martaba hai,*
> *Marad ishq da bhala ranjool mian*
> *Khule tinhan de bab kaloob andar*
> *Jinhan kita hai ishq kabool mian*

> First recite the praise for Khuda,
> For love is the root of the universe, O'friend!
> At the beginning Allah was the lover, and
> Prophet-messenger, the beloved, O'friend!
> Love marks the saint and the ascetic,
> Love is the honor of humans, O'friend!
> Those who welcome love within,
> Their hearts open to infinite realms, O'friend!

Their primal divine relationship opens up the horizon for human protagonists. In love the heart unlocks and takes lovers to those depths of richness and fullness where there is freedom from every limitation and barrier. Love for the poets works out as that potent hormone which dissolves the individual ego and expands the pores so wide that we savor the Other – divine and human – with utmost bliss. It carries many physiological associations: "love came and spread like blood in my veins" wrote the celebrated Chishti poet Amir Khusrau (died 1325 CE). The holy Qur'an and the experience of the Prophet remain the constant inspiration for our Sufi poets. In a popularly quoted verse, Allah expresses love for humanity through the analogy of the jugular vein: "We are closer to him than his jugular vein" (Qur'an 50:16).

Furthermore, the poetry of Bullhe Shah and Waris Shah resounds with the love and gratitude for specific Sufi Saints revered as transmitters of mystical initiation coming down from the Prophet Muhammad. As in the case of the Chishti Sheikh Farid, the chain of saints perpetuates mystical love amongst their community members through distinct methods of initiation, recitation, and spiritual exercises within their *tariqa* (literally "the way," *tariqa* represents a Sufi order). For Bullhe Shah and Waris Shah there is an ontological link between Allah, the Prophet, the Sufi Master, and the poets themselves. Bullhe Shah says, "*phar murshid abad khudai ho/vicc masti beparvahi ho/bekhahish benavai ho/vicc dil de khub safai ho* – Find a Master, so become the slave of Khuda; be carefree in ecstasy;/Impoverish your cravings/Polish your heart sparkling clean" ("In a Word"). In this poem we find textual evidence that Bullhe Shah was a disciple of Inayat Shah who belonged to the Qadiri order that originated with the Sufi saint Abdul Qadiri Jilani of Baghdad. The poet distinguishes his "Master of masters belonging to Baghdad – *pir piran Baghdad asada*" from his more immediate "master seated in Lahore – *murshid takht Lahore*" ("In a Word"). Bullhe Shah's poetry is full of explicit as well as implicit references to his Master, who is represented as guide, spouse, friend, lord, or beloved.

Likewise, Waris Shah's paean on love is followed by his praise for the Prophet; the Prophet's friends, including the four Caliphs; and Sufi saints. His fifth stanza in the opening of *Heer* is devoted to Sheikh Farid. Having grown up near Pakpattan himself, Waris Shah expresses great respect for Sheikh Farid's literary and spiritual impact. He repeats the Chishti master's popular nickname, Ganj-I shakar ("sugar treasure") and comments, "With his advent in the Punjab, pain and sorrow departed" ("In Praise of Hazrat Sheikh Farid Shakar-Ganj"). In a variety of ways, our Sufi poets posit love as the dynamic intersection between Allah, the Prophet Muhammad, Sufi Masters, and humanity.

It is in the context of multidimensional love that Waris Shah frames his *qissa*. Emperor Akbar's Hindu courtier, Damodar Gulati, had popularized the story of Heer and Ranjha at the beginning of the seventeenth century. Numerous other versions of the story, including those of Hafiz Shah Mukbal, Piloo, and Hafiz Barkhurdar, were also in circulation. Waris Shah retells this classic tale of the star-crossed lovers that had been a part of the Punjab's written and oral tradition, and with a unique aesthetic sensibility, makes their archetypal romance into a masterpiece of Punjabi literature. The author acknowledges that his friends requested him to narrate "Heer's *qissa* of inebriating love." So it was for the purpose of entertainment that he took up the project, and he worked extremely hard to follow up on it for his audience. In fact he compares his literary labor to that of the legendary lover Farhad who manually hewed dangerous boulders to dig a canal so that he could win the hand of his beloved Shirin. The Persian Farhad appears to be an important figure on his artistic canvas, for Ranjha's shock at the loss of his beloved is also compared with that of Farhad. Since Farhad appears as an image both of the poet and of the protagonist, at some subconscious level, Waris Shah imagines himself as the lover of the legendary Heer.

The plot centers on the illicit love affair between the children of two village chiefs: Dhido, the youngest and favorite son of Mauju Ranjha, and Heer, the daughter of Chuchak Syal. Because his jealous brothers allot him barren land upon the death of their father, Dhido Ranjha is forced to leave his village of Takht Hazara in northwestern Punjab. As he sleeps in a boat after his departure, Heer happens to come across him and instantly falls madly in love. With her recommendation, Ranjha gets a job as a herdsman for her snobbish family in the village of Jhang on the river Chenab. Playing his flute while tending buffaloes in pastoral landscapes, the mischievous and seductive Ranjha has ample opportunity to meet with his beloved and her bevy of friends – much like Krishna dallying with Radha and the Gopis in Brindaban. But Heer's nasty uncle Kaido spies on them, and warns the parents of Heer's ignoble behavior. Chuchak and his wife Maliki are deeply ashamed of their daughter staining the family name, and marry her off against all her pleading to Saida Khera in the village of Rangpur.

Ranjha then disguises as an austere yogi from the Kanphat tradition, making a change from the Vaishnavite Krishna figure to a Shaivite ascetic. Followers of the Hindu god Shiva, the Kanphat yogis are distinguished by their split (*phat*) earlobes (*kan*), dangling earrings, and bodies smeared in ash. These Hindu figures impressed the medieval Indian imagination; they are widely present in the art and literature of the Muslims and the Sikhs. In fact, a memorable scene from a Mughal album on exhibit at the Chester Beatty has a Khanphat yogi sitting with a dog – an exquisite illustration of the analogy between the dog's devotion to his master and the yogi's for Shiva![19] Putting on the garb of a typical "Hindu" Kanphat yogi, the "Muslim" Ranjha with his dog-like fidelity follows his beloved to her marital village. Heer's sister-in-law Sahiti (herself in love with a Baloch merchant) is instrumental in Ranjha's secret rendezvous with Heer. As a result of her masterminding, both the couples manage to elope; however, Heer and Ranjha are caught. Through his yogic powers, Ranjha is able to win Heer back, and her parents consent to their marriage. Sadly, as she is waiting for her groom, an excited Heer is treacherously poisoned by her

natal family. Ranjha hears the news of his beloved's death and dies from
the shock.

Woven in this plot are complex emotions, moral aphorisms, biting
critiques, ironic twists, and brilliant depictions of the simple daily life of
the Punjabis. Along with the usual morning scenes of men ploughing,
women churning buttermilk, grinding flour, spinning against the rose
colored skies "bursting out in joy," Waris Shah intersperses scenes that we
rarely come across in poetry (like the men – who made love the night
before – running to wash themselves)! There is nothing that Waris Shah
misses out on. Even the smelly farts of the orthodox Mullahs are part of
his literary discourse. His language is at once sublime and vulgar. He
represents love in most lofty expressions; he compares love with diarrhea:
"once you get the runs, no doctor can stop them – whatever medicines in
the world they may prescribe" (*Heer Waris Shah*, p. 74). His heroine
indulges in this unusual anatomical simile to verbalize not only her
tenacity but also the sheer urgency of love. Waris Shah's rustic wit, his
humor, and his sarcasm make him an all time favorite of the Punjabis.

The character of Heer is particularly admirable. Though contemporary
feminists would find a great deal lacking in Heer, for her time and place
she is quite radical. A literary critic from Pakistan observes that Heer is
probably the only heroine in romantic literature, who had to face the
Shariat Court and hear the threat of flogging from the lips of a Qazi. Yet
"she refused to surrender her fundamental right – freedom to marry a
man of her own choice, the right recognized by Islam unambiguously."[20]
For Shafqat Tanveer Mirza, Heer based her arguement on the Qur'anic
principles. Clearly the heroine is an intelligent woman who knows her
rights, who claims them for herself, and discerns the abuse of religion for
the upkeep of social and economic values,

Waris Shah named the work *Heer*, after her alone. She drives the plot
and owns the epic. Within the framework of a patriarchal society, Waris
Shah releases Heer from the stereotypical male-female roles, and endows
her with a powerful personality. Heer's beauty far surpasses the dainty
rhetoric of romantic damsels: "Her eyebrows are arched like the bows of
Lahore... the kohl in her eyes digs in fiercely like the armies of the
Punjab... her gait is like that of an intoxicated elephant... her features are
honed like the calligraphy of book... beholding her face is like making a
pilgrimage during Laylat al-qadr..." (*Heer Waris Shah*, pp. 47–8). The
poet's similes betray not only a Sufi's reverence for the art of calligraphy
and the Laylat al-qadr ("Night of Might" when the holy Qur'an was first

revealed in the final days of Ramadan), but also his pride in the Punjab with its famed city of Lahore and its fierce armies.

Heer's physical strength is important for Waris Shah. In a rather amusing scene she takes on the lame Kaido (her uncle), who she deems as the source of conflict and heartbreaks. She approaches him deceptively, and then roaring at him like a lion, thrashes him on the ground. The simile of the washerman whacking a cotton-blanket (*khes*) against a board graphically describes the ease with which Heer accomplishes her feat ("Heer Whacks Kaido"). Later, her friends join in, and they beat him up again. The poet seems to really enjoy the despicable Kaido being thrashed by Heer and her friends.

Heer is mentally and emotionally sturdy. She seethes with passion and sexuality. Leprosy was common in that age, so in her courageous pledge for Ranjha she vows, "If ever I take another love, as a leper's let my eyes and life wither." She boldly stands up to her family, society, and religious leaders. To her father she asserts that Ranjha is Khuda's own gift to her and she is addicted to him: "This love-sickness is such that my life may go, but my love will not" ("Heer's Addiction"). She recommends Ranjha to her father, which gets him his job with her family: "*vasai nur allah da mukhre te, muhon rabb hi rabb citarda hai* – On his face dwells Allah's light; his lips recite *rabb*, and *rabb* alone" (*Heer Waris Shah*, p. 56). Qur'anic epithets for the Divine – Khuda, Allah, Rabb emerge in Heer's introduction of her lover, whose inner devotion radiates externally, and spiritual exercises (*dhikr*) slip out incessantly. A determined Heer reiterates her resolve to her mother: "*na murangi ranjare ton bhaven bap de bap da bap ave* – I will not turn away from Ranjha even if father's father's father were to come in my way" ("Enough Mother"). In a dynamic repetition, Heer audaciously rejects the rules coming down from the fathers.

The daughter conveys a moral sense to the mother who blindly follows androcenric codes. By warning her against the murder of daughters, Heer tries to awaken Maliki from the stupor of false consciousness: "*jinhan betian marian roz kiamat/sir tinhan de vadda gunah mae/milan khanian tinhan nun phar kar ke/jivain marian je tivain khah mae –* Those who kill their daughters/Are heavily fined on the Judgment Day;/They are served the flesh torn from their victims/Just what they destroyed that is what they must eat, O mother" (*Heer Waris Shah*, p. 73). Heer reiterates Sheikh Farid's central theme of the Day of Judgment, but she undergirds it with a profound social awareness of injustice against women. In her dialogues she denounces conventional beliefs and practices centered on external authorities and outward response. Tracing her intoxication to the Divine source, Heer uses Qur'anic expressions and concepts to affirm passionate love as the sole religious practice. With her Sufi infused vocabulary she too – like the poets from the Guru Granth – espouses fundamental human principles. Of course Heer's family did not hear her arguments then, and neither has Heer's patriarchal Indo-Pak society to date.

It is curious that the very episodes of Heer disputing with the Qazi and her mother would be most popular in late nineteenth-century India! As noted by Farina Mir, the texts of several poets focus on just one or two of Heer's exchanges.[21] Why would Heer's emotional tenacity, her robust language, and her defiance of religious and societal authorities, continue to capture the imagination of the male poets and their patriarchal society? Where docile and submissive women are cherished, why would Heer's trenchant words be printed and read and performed over and over? There is no one answer to this complex dynamic. Mir's thesis that despite their divisive political context, the texts articulate a piety "all Punjabis could participate in" certainly accounts for their popularity.[22] And yes in a colonial climate in which caretakers of mosques, mandirs, and gurdwaras were misusing their offices (we will encounter the abuse by the caretakers of gurdwaras in the next chapter) Heer's harsh critique of the Qazi would have resonated well. But I would add that there is something radically free spirited about Heer, which precisely in the politically repressive context of the Raj, would have special appeal for the Punjabis. But then again Heer's devotion could simply be flattering for males, since a woman is ready to renounce everything for her man (something a heart-broken Waris Shah had desperately desired)? Or it could give them the sadistic pleasure of pitting a mother against her own daughter? At the metaphoric level, Heer's rejection of religious authorities (embodied by the Qazi) and societal codes (embodied by the mother) to endorse the unorthodox Sufi path would work out very well in the diverse Province of the Punjab where Sufism was popular amongst Muslim, Hindu, and Sikh audiences. Forty thousand pilgrims squeezing through the "door of Paradise" at Sheikh Farid's mausoleum in an evening in June 1911 testifies to the Sufi prominence in the region.[23]

Heer's daring speeches and deeds are depicted throughout the narrative text. With her sister-in-law Sahiti's support, Heer clandestinely meets with her lover, and even feigns a snake-bite so the yogi with occult powers (Ranjha in disguise) would be brought over. Heer demonstrates superb dramatic skills: she clenches her teeth, twists her body into a knot, she goes into concussions, and turns her eyes "blue and yellow." The family is convinced that Heer has been bitten by the most venomous of snakes, and bring in all sorts of physicians and snake charmers to cure her. They try countless antidotes, but all in vain. Heer and Sahiti's strategy succeeds: their family calls upon the "yogi" (disguised Ranjha), and together the lovers manage to run away. All along Heer thinks, speaks, walks, and does everything in accordance with her desire. Heer's authentic subjectivity is quite an anomaly in her sexist Punjabi society that has idealized docile and submissive women who live entirely for their husbands and their families, without any desire of their own. In breathtaking imagery, Waris Shah depicts his fiery heroine:

> … A peacock she dances seductively,
> An elephant in heat she plunges ahead,
> Killing every naïve fellow on the way…
>
> ("Preparations")

The more we read Waris Shah, the more we realize that Heer's confidence and empowerment are a direct result of her being in touch with her erotic self.

But Waris Shah is equally good at disclosing the rampant subjugation and victimization of women. In the Punjabi patriarchal social structure, family honor (*izzat*) is centered on the bodies and sexuality of women. Control over the daughter's reproductive rights leads to the reproduction of her family's identity and prestige. Religious and social rules conflate as the Qazi and her mother-brother-father exhort Heer to marry the suitor of their choice. Heer's escapades with Ranjha bring much disgrace to the upperclass Syals. The poet quotes the parents asking: Why did we not strangle her at birth? Give her poison? Drown her in a well? Float her away? ("Why did we Not?"). The father's regret for losing out on the manifold opportunities to kill his fearless daughter brings a chuckle to the eavesdropping reader. But it also makes the stomach churn. How easy it is to kill a baby daughter! How men and women internalize and perpetuate horrific sexist values! How the mother in her false consciousness is an equal partner in the brutal practices of honor killing and infanticide! Such a conversation in Heer's family brings home the stark reality of women who are being killed by their families right at this moment in the name of "honor" – only because they fell in love with somebody of their own choice. They explain the dwindling population of baby girls due to sex-specific abortions eliminating female fetuses. The conversation also serves as a tragic foreshadowing of her family's ultimate victory – their poisoning of Heer just when she is happily awaiting Ranjha's wedding party. A radical heroine has no place in society.

As in the case of Bullhe Shah, many of Waris Shah's passages could very well have been composed today. We hear him incisively criticize the suffocating and oppressive custom of veiling. Instead of *burqa* he uses the north Indian word *ghundh* for veil, which is found in Punjabi, Hindi, and Urdu. Waris Shah does not merely see it as a piece of material with which women cover their hair, their faces and their bodies, but as a bundle of complex norms involving patriarchal control of female sexuality. He compares this abusive female practice to putting birds in a cage. The poet poignantly declares, "The world opens up when the veil slips down." Waris Shah's imperative *"agg laike ghundh nun sarieh ni* – let us burn the veil in the fire" ("Burn the Veil") bears a striking resonance with that of the contemporary radically feminist Muslim, Taslima Nasrin, who is famous for her slogan, "Let's Burn the Burqa."

Sadly, the loud exhortations of our Sufi poets have gone unheard. As our subsequent poets Dhani Ram Chatrik, Firoz Din Sharaf, and Amrita Pritam show us, religious conflicts abound in the Punjab. Sexism festers. Infanticide (in the form of gender-selective abortions) is widespread. Many women continue to wear the veil, and those who do not still live as though they were encaged – being excluded from the public sphere, and from political and economic processes and interactions. For centuries Punjabis have read and recited the verse of Bullhe Shah and Waris Shah without receiving their empowering message. Gadamer's remarks on tradition help us understand the cause for this terrible lack of communication: "It is the tyranny of hidden prejudices that makes us deaf to what speaks to us in tradition."[24] Traditional values – both positive and negative – are passed down orally and aurally. In order to hear our poets, the auditory canal has to be clear of all muffling prejudices. We readers need to switch on our minds and put off the cultural norms that have made us deaf to the language of our poets. In joy of the earthy humor and beauty of the landscapes portrayed by our poets, Punjabis dance till they drop; in sympathy with Heer, Punjabis drown themselves in oblivion. But they do nothing to transform their social reality. We need to hone our aural faculties so that when their words strike our ears, they are actually heard. Bullhe Shah was wise enough to know that people hear without understanding, and so he alerts:

> *bansi sabh koi sune sunave*
> *arth is da koi virala pave*

> Everybody hears and plays the notes of your flute
> But rarely does anybody grasp their meaning!
>   ("Krishna Plays the Magic Flute")

I hope that my readers will respond to my translations of these visionary poets by taking some individual responsibility for eliminating the horribly contagious diseases of sexism, sectarianism, and snobbery.

Bullhe Shah

౭ ౨

Love Spells

With magic and spells,
   I'll win my beloved.
First I'll recite a charm, and then
   With the flame of the sun,
I'll light it up.

With magic and spells,
   I'll win my beloved.
With liner in my eyes,
Eyelashes like clouds,
   I'll blow those flames high.

With magic and spells,
   I'll win my beloved.
I'll use no other means,
   I'll brace myself
With my bare youth.

With magic and spells,
   I'll win my beloved.
Crossing the seven oceans of my heart,
   I'll churn out a raging tide.

With magic and spells,
*   I'll win my beloved.*
I'll explode into lightning,
And fiercely dance
Around ominous clouds.

With magic and spells,
*   I'll win my beloved.*
In the furnace of my love,
I'll exorcise evil spirits:
I'll toss in the stars
Like *harmal* seeds,
And burn them up
Like the heat of the sun.

With magic and spells,
*   I'll win my beloved.*
Neither married, nor virgin,
    I'll nurse my child in my lap.

With magic and spells,
*   I'll win my beloved.*
On the path of Bullhe Shah,
    I'll sit and sing my lyrics;

With magic and spells,
*   I'll win my beloved.*

A Needle without a Thread

How can we love without physical love?
How can a needle sew without thread?
Physical love is a blessing –
Spinning everything into ecstasy.

As love seeps into the marrow,
We die living our very best.
Love is our father and mother,
Love spins everything into ecstasy.

A lover's body may age, yet here
I stand in the shadow
    Of my moon-like beloved
Watching lovers laugh with gusto.
    Love teaches us to cross all rules, so
Those who are suffused with its flow
    They are utterly helpless
Their every cell melts with rapture.

There is no secret whatsoever:
The Divine is seen everywhere!
O Bullah, lovers thus swim across.
Those who recall their lover's abode,
The Divine sees and speaks to them
Even peeks into their inner self
And spins everything into ecstasy.

How can we love without physical love?
How can a needle sew without thread?

Frying in the Pan

O friend, I am struck by eternal love
That love from the beginning of time
It is frying me in a pan
The fried is being fried over again!
O friend, I am struck by primal love
That love from the beginning of time.

It kills the dead over and over
It crushes the crushed over and over!
O I am struck by eternal love
That love from the beginning of time.

My skin is burning like straw on fire
My inside is stinging with thorns!
O I am struck by eternal love
That love from the beginning of time.

The arrow of love has struck my heart
But it won't move despite all motion!
O I am struck by eternal love
That love from the beginning of time.

Bullhe Shah's love is unique
It does not dissolve
    No matter how much you mix it!
O I am struck by eternal love
That love from the beginning of time.

Why Turn to the Ka'ba?

Why must I turn towards the Ka'ba,
When my heart longs for Takht Hazara?

People say their prayers facing Ka'ba,
I say my prayers facing my lover;
My heart longs for Takht Hazara!

If you find any flaws in me, dear Ranjha,
Don't forget my deeds flow from my desire –
My heart longs for Takht Hazara!

Untrained, I don't know how to swim –
My savior, shame would be yours if I drown
My heart longs for Takht Hazara!

I have not found anybody your equal,
Though I have searched the world over;
My heart longs for Takht Hazara!

Bullhe Shah says: love is exceptional;
It redeems the worthless.
Why must I turn towards the Ka'ba,
When my heart longs for Takht Hazara?

All Forgotten

Fasts, pilgrimage, prayers, O mother,
    My beloved came and made me forget!

When I heard the news of my lover
I forgot all about logic and syntax
As he struck the soundless chord
Fasting, pilgrimage, prayers, O mother
My beloved made me forget them all!

When my lover entered my home
I forgot the *sharia* and its laws
I see my lover in each and every thing
    That radiance sparkling inside and out
How can people not see!

Fasting, pilgrimage, prayers O mother
My beloved has made me forget them all!

My Friend Taught Me One Letter

My friend taught me one letter
My friend taught me one letter
Ain and Ghain have the same shape –
Except for the dot of a diacritic
Which creates such an uproar!
My friend taught me one letter
In order to steal Sassi's heart,
That One took on the form of Punnu.
My friend taught me one letter
Bullhe Shah says: I have no caste, for
All of me has become my master, Shah Inayat.
My friend taught me one letter

In a Word

To sum it up in a word
Hold on to the word,
    Give up your calculations
        Get rid of your blasphemous talks;
Free yourself from diseases that cling to the grave
        Fill your heart with pure dreams;
Just the perfect thing for our entire life,
        Can be summed up in a word.
Why then rub your nose on the ground?
        Why prostrate before the *mihrab*?
Why read prayers out loud
        That you do not understand?
Can the truth ever be hidden?
        It can be summed up in one word.
Many return from doing the Hajj
        They wear blue around their necks
They barter their pilgrimage for naught
        And we call this experience good?
Can the truth ever be hidden?
        It can be summed up in one word.
Many wander in forests
        Living on a grain of food per day
Needlessly they exhaust themselves
        Searching outside what they possess within.
Why waste ourselves fasting for forty days when
        We can gain all profits from but one word!
Find a master, became the slave of Khuda,
        Be carefree in ecstasy;
Impoverish your cravings
        Polish your heart sparkling clean.
Asks Bullhe: can truth ever be blocked?
        It can be summed up in a word!

Language of Silence

Such is my enlightenment:
Hindu or Muslim is irrelevant.
I accept only the name of love,
It's the lover who conquers all.
Such is my enlightenment:
Hindu or Muslim is irrelevant.

See how villains make such noise
    They turn birth and death into rituals
Fools fall prey to their shouts,
The lover reveals us the truth.
Such is my enlightenment:
Hindu or Muslim is irrelevant.

O Bullhe, feeling of love is unique
Love is so savory and spicy!
The fools get lost in words;
Poets speak in silence.
Such is my enlightenment:
Hindu or Muslim is irrelevant.

Out of Tune, Out of Step

Those touched by perfect love,
They dance out of tune
　　They dance out of step.

Do not disturb the distressed,
Let them suffer their anguish;
They escape birth and death,
They know themselves.
Those touched by perfect love,
They dance out of tune
　　They dance out of step.

Those who wear the robe of love,
They receive the *fatwa*
　　From the divine court;
As they sip the cup of revelation,
Their questions and doubts die out.
Those touched by perfect love,
They dance out of tune
　　They dance out of step.

In whom dwells the divine,
They jump up calling,
　　"Beloved! O' Beloved!"
They do not care for rules
　　They do not care for tunes,
They play their own sports.
Those touched by perfect love,
They dance out of tune
　　They dance out of step.

　　　　O Bullah, I have found
　　　　　　My lover's true town,
　　　　Din and falsity have fizzled out;
　　　　For truthful people I tell the truth:
　　　　I see immaculate light.
　　　　Those touched by perfect love,
　　　　They dance out of tune,
　　　　　　They dance out of step.

Neither Sinners nor Saints

We are not Hindu, we are not Muslim,
So let us give up our pride, and do our spinning;
We are neither Sunni nor Shia;
We are a family, so let us live in harmony.

We are not hungry,
    we are not full;
We are not naked,
    we have no clothes;
We are not crying,
    we are not happy;
We are not deserted;
    we have no home.

We are not sinners, we are not saints,
I do not know of sin, I do not know of sainthood;
Says Bullhe: when we are in tune with the Divine,
Hindu and Muslim lose their difference.

Topsy-Turvy Goes the World

Topsy-turvy goes the world:
Crows hunt eagles,
        Sparrows eat hawks;
Strong Iraqi horses
        Are badly whipped,
Good for nothing donkeys
        Are richly fed.
Says Bullhe, who can stop
        This order from high up?
Topsy-turvy goes the world!

Clay We Are

We bounce because of this clay my friend
How lovely the clay full of flowers!

The horse is made of clay,
    Its saddle blanket is of clay,
    Its rider is clay as well.
Clay generates clay. Our cosmos
    Echoes with the sound of clay,
Clay also destroys clay
    With weapons made of clay;
The clay full of itself
    Is proud.

Clay is the garden, clay are the plants,
        Clay is the entire vegetation;
Clay has come to admire clay, but
        The beautiful spring of the lush clay –
After laughing and playing – to clay it returns,
        To lie with its legs stretched out.
Says Bullhe: if you solve this riddle,
You'll lighten the burden on your shoulders.

Come Meet Me Now

I will be going forever to my in-laws' home,
O my friends, so come meet me now!
Allah willing, you too will be going,
O do come and meet me now.

Different thorns in different hues
    Will seize me soon. Of course
I'll take with me my sorrows from this world
    But those of the next, to whom will I relinquish?
Foremost is the pain of parting from my friends
    Like that of the crane forsaken by her flock.

My parents have given me
    A skirt and a scarf,
Now that I think about my dowry
    I shed big hot tears;
My mother-in-law and new sisters
    Will taunt me for sure.
Bullhe knows our sovereign shields us –
    So help me pass over this calamity;
Since I fail to receive your justice,
    Shower me with your benevolence.

I will be going forever to my in-laws' home,
O my friends, so come meet me now!
Allah willing, you too will be going,
O do come and meet me now.

Show Me the Way

I am smitten by true love, O
Show me the way to my Beloved!
I was a naïve little girl in my parents' home,
When he stole my heart away, O
Show me the way to my Beloved!
I studied logic, grammar, laws, and texts
       But I am bereft of love, O
Show me the way to my Beloved!
Those who drink from the cup of love
       What do they care about fasts or prayers? O
Show me the way to my Beloved!
Says Bullhe: when I sat with the Divine,
       All rituals and discipline left me. O
Show me the way to my Beloved!

Stubborn

Stubborn is my name O friends
The Mullah taught me lessons
But I learned nothing beyond *alif*
I was thrashed with his shoe.
Stubborn is my name

How I fixed my eyes on you! To undo
My friends came to beat me
My father and mother joined in too.
Stubborn is my name O friends

My in-laws refused to let me in
My own parents kicked me out
I have no place in my natal home
Stubborn is my name O friends

They all force me to study
They won't let me be
O friends who should I go to?
Stubborn is my name O friends
O Beloved, what have you done to me!
Says Bullhe: I wish my sickness upon you
– Only then will you dispense justice.
Stubborn is my name O friends

Our Beloved Has Come

Our beloved has come to my house

Wondrous sounds of unicity fill the air
Unstruck melody flows from the flute
I have gained the spiritual seat in Lahore
Our beloved has come to my house

As true love blazes high,
My vices burn to ash;
I am in the lap of my beloved
Our beloved has come to my house

How could I be trapped by time, when
I am addicted to the timeless cup of wine?
I have forgotten my caste and name
Our beloved has come to my house

What's the use of gaining fifty from twenty
When I can have a glimpse of my beloved?
The entire world is flushed with radiance
Our beloved has come to my house

Now all I want is to be held tightly!
Says Bullhe Shah: he has come to us
So my desire is fulfilled
Our beloved has come to my house

Ranjha Is Here

Come my friends,
Join together to congratulate me,
I have found my beloved Ranjha.

Today is blessed, for
Ranjha has entered my home.
He holds a staff in his hands,
He wears a shawl around his neck,
He looks just like a cowherd.

Come my friends,
Join together to congratulate me!

His crown is lost amidst the cows
He wanders in woods and forests
People forgetful of Allah
Do not recognize Reality.

Come my friends,
Join together to congratulate me!

Says Bullhe Shah I made a deal:
I drank a cup of poison
I did not consider any profit or loss
I hauled off a bundle of sorrows.

Come my friends,
     Join together to congratulate me!

Krishna Plays the Magic Flute

Krishna plays the magic flute
O Ranjha with the flute –
    O cowherd Ranjha!
You are in tune
    With all of us!
You make your delights
    Chime with our consciousness
Krishna plays the magic flute

O flute player,
    You are called Krishna
You are our virtue
    You are our inner self
Yet our eyes cannot quite see you!
    How complex your sport.
Krishna plays the magic flute

Everybody hears and plays the notes of your flute,
    But rarely does anybody grasp their meaning;
Whoever hears its unstruck sound,
    Your flute mesmerizes that person.
Krishna plays the magic flute

Hearing your melodious flute,
    Mind and body cry out like peacocks;
Your rhythmic twists and turns reveal
    That solo note sustaining your great art.
Krishna plays the magic flute

This flute has a long writ
    If we search we can find it
Simple is its style for it has gathered
        Its attributes from its essential Being.
Krishna plays the magic flute

This flute has some five or seven stars
    Each plays its own part
The one note that vibrates in all
    It has blown away our senses.
Krishna plays the magic flute

Says Bullhe: end all this conflict
    Welcome friends to the door
Do keep your deal with the Kalma,
    So the Master will stand as your witness.
Krishna plays the magic flute

Heer Is Ranjha

Calling out Ranjha Ranjha, O friend,
    I became Ranjha myself!
Call me Dhido Ranjha,
    I am Heer no more.
Ranjha is in me, I am in Ranjha
    There is no other reality;
I am not, he alone exists
    He does what he wishes.
Calling out Ranjha Ranjha, O friend,
    I became Ranjha myself!

In my hand is a staff, I follow a herd of cattle
    A tan shawl wraps my shoulders;
Says Bullhe, look at Heer of Syal
    What she has come to be!
Calling out Ranjha Ranjha, O friend,
    I became Ranjha myself!
Call me Dhido Ranjha,
    I am Heer no more.

There is a Thief in my Shawl

There is a thief in my shawl
Who should I call to alert O saints
There is a thief in my shawl

1

Here Ram Das, there Fateh Muhammad –
    So goes the ancient brawl;
Muslims scorn the crematory fire,
    Hindus scorn the grave;
Fights and arguments go on
    While somebody else escapes.
Who should I call to alert O saints
There is a thief in my shawl

2

The One I searched for
    I did not find;
But a person sought by
    The Divine is strong.
The writ on our forehead
    Who can break or tear it?
Who should I call to alert O saints
There is a thief in my shawl

3

Our ancestral master is in Baghdad,
    My master's seat is in Lahore
But we are all the same:
    The kite and the string are the same.
Keep this in mind, I tell you,
    Bullhe Shah spreads this news.
Who should I call to alert O saints
There is a thief in my shawl

Bullah Wonders Who He Is

Bullah wonders who he is

I am not seated with the pious in the mosque
   I am not sinking in acts of vice;
I am not with the pure
   I am not with the polluted;
I am not Moses
   I am not Pharaoh
Bullah wonders who he is

I do not follow Indian scriptures
   I do not follow Western scriptures;
I do not take drugs
   I do not take alcohol;
I am not decadent
   Nor licentious;
I am neither asleep
   Nor awake
Bullah wonders who he is

I am neither happy
   Nor am I sad
I am not clean
   I am not dirty
I am neither on land
   Nor in the sea
I am not made of fire
   I am not made of air
Bullah wonders who he is

I do not belong to Arabia
   I do not belong to Lahore
I am not from the city
   Nor from the district of Nagaur
I am not Hindu
   I am not Muslim
I am not from Peshawar

I do not live in Nadaun
Bullah wonders who he is

I do not know the mystery of faith
    I am not the child of Adam and Eve
I have no name for myself
    I am not among the settled or the migrants
Bullah wonders who he is

From A to Z –
    All of that I am;
Anybody else,
    I do not perceive;
More intelligent than me
    There is no one.
Asks Bullah: Who is the Sovereign?
    Who stands there?
Bullah wonders who he is

But Bullah: who stands there?
    Is that the Sovereign?

Waris Shah

ॐ ॐ

Praise

First recite the praise for Khuda,
For love is the root of the universe, O'friend!
At the beginning Allah was the lover, and
Prophet-messenger, the beloved, O'friend!
Love marks the saint and the ascetic,
Love is the honor of humans, O'friend!
Those who welcome love within,
Their hearts open to infinite realms, O'friend!

In Praise of Hazrat Sheikh Farid Shakar-Ganj

Maudud's endearing saint Chishti –
Masud, Sugar Treasure, – abides everywhere;
He marks the excellence of the Chishti clan,
He has made his city Pakpattan famous;
This saint is the zenith of perfection,
His humility and piety are renowned;
With his advent in the Punjab,
Pain and sorrow departed.

Request from my Friends

My friends came and asked me:
Compose a new *qissa* on Heer;
Narrate in a delicious tongue
Her *qissa* of inebriating love;
In lyrics of magical spring,
Paint the union of Heer and Ranjha
So we may all sit together and enjoy
The thrill of Heer's passion.

Magical Romance

Accepting the request of my friends
I have composed this magical narrative;
I synchronized the lyrics as
A strewn new rose is recreated.
I labored with great travail of my spirit –
A Farhad hewing boulders for his love;
With choicest selections I created
This perfume distilled from the rarest rose.

Break of Dawn

With the song of sparrows
    Travelers set out
Blenders plunge into yogurt pots
Pure dawn spreads her radiance
The pinks burst out in clamorous joy.
Ploughmen take their oxen out
    To dig the land and sow the seeds;
Ladies bring out their hand mills
    To grind the flour they'll knead and bake;
Young women sit at their spinning wheels,
    The whole world is arrested in chores;
Those who spent the night making love
    They run for water to bathe themselves.
Ranjha set out and came to the river
    To find the ferry overcrowded
– With the big fat Ludden
    Sitting like a barrel of honey in a shop.

Preparations

Heer bathes herself, she dresses up in silks,
She massages her hair with scented oils;
She twists up her seductive braids,
Coaxing a few wisps around her fair face.
Eyes with liner, laden with lust,
She gets ready with her weapons of beauty.
She cleanses her face with a mask,
    On her lips she puts crimson red –
Coating them anew over and over.
She covers her head with a diaphanous scarf,
She decks her ears with big dangling hoops,
Her brocade bodice fits her snug and tight,
Her bangles chime, her jewels sparkle.
With anklets haughtily jingling,
Her forehead glowing with gold and red,
Heer from the Syal family saunters over.
A peacock, she dances seductively,
An elephant in heat, she plunges ahead,
Killing every naïve fellow on the way.
Eyes intoxicating, lips lethal with red bark,
A fairy arrives jingle jangling.
At times she veils her face
At times she shows her face –
    Striking her beholders dead.
Lifting off her veil, a sensual Heer,
Tries to win her lover again;
To the master who owns her pleasure,
She shows off her treasures one by one.

Take Hold of your Savings

When Heer took off her veil,
And showed her face,
Ranjha lost his wits and senses;
With just a flash of her beauty,
The Lanka garden fairy
Tore apart the heart of her lover.

"My cruel parents forced me into marriage,
But your love burns me to ashes;
I forgot my parents and the rest of my kin,
I am wedded only to my beloved cowherd.
My limbs have touched nobody but you;
God stands as my witness here.
Take hold of your savings, fresh and unspent,
My desire for you burns my heart."

Allah knows how these two lovers
Sacrificed all delights;
Asks Waris Shah, why did you
Put them on this path of anguish?

Meeting in the Garden

She first touched his feet
 In the customary way
But then she
 Fiercely embraced him.
A great new wonder
 Came to sight –
The flame shoots
 Towards the moth.
What magic!
 Light blazed
News flashed
 Hearts thundered.
O friends, the *Jatti* Heer,
 Like a thief's sesame sweet
Robbed her lover
 With a single kiss.
Intoxicated, he started
 To ramble feverishly,
The pen of an ascetic
 Started to flow.
From the smoldering heat of the yogi,
 Ignited flames began to soar.
The lovers met
 In the stealth of the garden,
Their simple meeting
 Caught the world's attention.
Says Waris, the Divine
 Unites separated hearts;
Look how the fairy
  Clings to her clown!

Heer Whacks Kaido

Heer hurried to meet him on the way
Pretending to address him amiably at first
But coming closer she roared like a lion
With drops of anger flooding her cheeks
She pulled his cap from his head
She wrenched his locket
From round his neck
Grabbing him by the waist
She threw Kaido
On the ground in rage
Like a washerman whacks *khes* against a board!
    Says Waris Shah, an angel from the heavens
    Pitched Satan down on the floor!

Heer's Pledge of Love

I swear upon my father, O Ranjha,
Upon my mother too,
    I will never leave you!
Without you, life is sin for me,
My eyes will meet no man's body.
I swear by saint Khwaja Khizr,
I am a pig if I break my pledge of love;
If ever I take another lover,
Let my eyes and life, like a leper's, wither.

Why Did We Not

Kuchak asks his wife Maliki,
Why did we not strangle her at birth?
Why did we not give her a drop of poison,
Which today would have been our savior?
Why did we not drown her in some deep well?
Why did we not float her away in the river?
Says Waris, with the fear of Khuda,
Why did we not lay her to rest
    In the bed of the river Karun?

Heer's Addiction

Says Heer, dear father, addicts
Cannot live without their drug;
I cannot live without Ranjha, sir,
Incorrigible habits do not change.
Lions and leopards can't live without meat
With a single pounce they earn their meal.
I made my wish for Ranjha at the *dargah*
– The herdsman is Khuda's own blessing!
A gift written in my destiny
How can anybody erase it?
Such is my love-sickness that
Life may go, but love will not.

Says the Father

Pull out her braids, cut off her hair
Wring her neck and bury her far below
Crack her head with the churn
Break her back with the club
Take a sickle – tear open her stomach
And gouge her eyes with those needles.

No way will she turn away from him
Says Waris, try as much as we may!

Enough Mother

Mother, it's enough! Curse no more!
        Cursing incurs grave demerits.
To dishonor what is Divine is horrible,
        We sin when we kill our daughters.
May some fever or plague take me
        Away from this wretched place
But I will not turn away from Ranjah
Even if father's father's father
        Were to come in my way.

Punjabi Noah

Hurled away from his beloved Heer,
    Ranjha was in utter shock.
He felt pushed away
    From his paradise –
Like Adam expelled
    From the Garden of Eden,
Like Satan
    Pushed away by God.
Was he Shaddad
    Banned from heaven?
Or king Nimrud
    Destroyed by a mosquito?
Says Waris Shah,
    This lover was utterly bewildered
Like Noah caught in the Flood.

To Ranjha and Heer
Blessings from the Five Pirs

Now you both must remember Rabb;
Never must you put a blemish on love.
May you have *churi* to eat,
And milk from the choicest buffalo;
Never must you waver in thought or deed.
By remembering Khuda each segment of the day,
May you earn praise and honor.
    Says Waris Shah the five saints urged:
    O children, never ever put love to shame!

Burn the Veil

This veil is full of woes,
So burn it away!
It hides the glory of beauty,
It shows the abuse of woman.
The veil sinks the ship of lovers,
It suffocates lovers like birds in a cage.
The world opens up
When the veil slips down.
A veil blinds even those with eyes,
So take it off your face, young one!
Says Waris Shah, do not bury pearls,
    Nor set the flower on fire.

Heer Feigns a Snake Bite

With her teeth clenched,
    Heer tightens her limbs into a knot
She twists her lips, and
    Drains her cheeks blue.
Her nostrils flare
    As she loudly sobs
Her eyes turning
    Blue and yellow,
In spasms she cries,
    "I am dying."
Her limbs jerk
    Unconsciously, and
In those violent convulsions,
    She gasps for life.
The devil and his companions
    Bow in humility –
Proclaiming Sahiti [Heer's sister-in-law]
    A teacher unsurpassed.

Healing Heer

Heer's inlaws, the Kheras, called countless exorcists,
    Along with physicians and snake charmers.
These experts were equipped with Plato's supreme cure,
    And antidotes by Western alchemists.
They had myriad types of snakes
    Tucked in their baskets to cast their spells;
They had onions, amulets, incense, cowries,
    And thread spun by virgin hands.
Somebody gave Heer milk of the *akk* plant
    Another gave her onions to eat
Another gave her betel-nut, and yet another
    Brought her beads soaked in buttermilk.
Then a curtain was drawn, and Heer was separated
    From the gathering of men and women;
She received oil, chilies, herbs, milk, coins, and
    Butter, – but
    All in vain.
Says Waris Shah, snake charmers thronged the village,
Ready with their antidotes to cure a Heer "poisoned."

Sahiti Suggests

Sahiti said, there is no effect whatsoever
Heer's snakebite resists all spells.
A yogi has come in the Black Garden,
Even his footsteps are known to cure all ills.
Poisonous snakes, frogs, vipers, leopards –
All of them pay homage to him.
Crowned cobras, winged wasps, water-
Snakes, pythons, – dread him alike.
Not the slightest sorrow or pain remains,
His magic expels all spirits and ghosts.
Whoever meets him
Is healed forever;
Diseases from generations
Are cured in a flash;
Kings, queens, demons, spirits, and fairies,
Come to him to peer into their future.
Where all other physicians fail,
O Waris Shah, this yogi triumphs!

3

MODERN POETS

The modern poets Bhai Vir Singh (1872–1957), Dhani Ram Chatrik (1876–1954), and Firoz Din Sharaf (1898–1955) brought a revolutionary transformation in the Punjabi language. Born after the annexation of the Punjab in 1849, they witnessed the violent effect of the politics of language provoked by the Raj. Persian had been introduced as the court language as early as the reign of Mahmud of Ghazna, and so it remained through the Delhi Sultanate, the Mughal Empire, and the Sikh Kingdom of Lahore. At the informal level, however, the majority of the people spoke a mixture of Punjabi dialects without distinctions of religion, class, or caste, and they shared the vital literary heritage of the Punjabi language. The numerous linguistic maps, reports, and district gazetteers produced by the colonial state, and even the census of the Punjab conducted in 1881, repeatedly confirmed Punjabi as the primary spoken language of the Punjab, with figures in some districts ranging from 85 to 98 percent.[1] Subsequently under the Raj, language became a radically divisive issue. In the context of the Punjab, Bernard Cohn's thesis is especially applicable: "The vast social world that was India had to be classified, categorized, and bounded before it could be ordered" (in the chapter on the Command of Language and the Language of Command).[2] With the British victory in the Anglo-Sikh wars, the rich heterogeneous linguistic world of pre-colonial Punjab was conquered by "a discourse of differentiations" and reduced to homolingual units: Urdu, Hindi, Punjabi.

Missionary activity was extended to cover the newly acquired territory and it received government patronage. The Christian enterprise also penetrated into spheres of social welfare such as education and medical care. With the famous Wood's Despatch of 1854, the government started opening schools and colleges for the diffusion of Western art, science, philosophy and literature, but it made it a "sacred duty" to promote education in both English and the vernacular languages.[3] Such activities initiated a new process of literary, social, cultural, and religious resurgence amongst the Indians. In the north Indian landscape, three powerful movements of reform and renewal were generated: the Arya Samaj in Hinduism, the Aligarh in Islam, and the Singh Sabha in Sikhism.

The Arya Samaj founded by Swami Dayanand in 1875 was a vigorous Hindu reform movement, which exerted tremendous impact in the Punjab. Promoting the progressive way of the Vedas as the "original religion" of the Aryas, it condemned practices it deemed had accrued over the centuries: polytheism, idolatry, animal sacrifice, ancestor worship, and child marriage. In Islam, Sir Syed Ahmed Khan launched the "Aligarh" movement to reinterpret its teachings in order to meet the demands of the new age. It initially began in 1875 as a secondary school patterned after European models, and soon became a very influential modernizing movement in Islam on the Indian subcontinent. The Singh Sabha issued from the deliberations of leading Sikhs of the time such as Thakur Singh Sandhanwalia, Baba Sir Khem Singh Bedi, and Kanwar Bikrama Singh of Kapurthala who met in Amritsar in 1873. Less than a year old at that time, Bhai Vir Singh eventually became its most ardent exponent and eloquent spokesman. The Singh Sabha aimed at recapturing the original message of the Gurus and recovering and re-establishing Sikh identity. As Arvind Mandair claims in *The Specter of the West*, the two-pronged colonial machine enforced a symbolic order on the colonized peoples, and made the indigenous elites psychologically receptive to its categories and polarizations.[4]

The colonial state's repressive legislations combined with the indigenous reform movements unleashed an exclusivist force in the Punjab. Sectarian divisions came into play as never before, and language became a crucial marker of religious identity. The British patronized Urdu, a Persianized form of the common language based on the Khari Boli dialect of Delhi.[5] It did not matter much in their deliberations that the majority of the population was Punjabi-speaking in the province, and that the Punjabi-speakers had valiantly defended English establishments and families during the 1857 Mutiny in the "Urdu speaking" localities of the United Provinces and Delhi. Punjabi farmers were even cultivating tea for the Empire in their northern regions. In a letter by the Commissioner and Superintendent of the Delhi Division to the Secretary of the Punjab Government surface colonial state's prejudices and insecurities:

It will be a stultification of our whole education system to adopt Punjabee as our Court language. Here we are teaching the population to read and write Oordoo... Besides, I think that any measure which would revive the Goormukhee, which is the written Punjabee tongue would be a political error...[6]

Limiting the language to the Sikhs, administrators described Punjabi as "barbarous dialect" (John Lawrence, Chief Commissioner) with its "degenerating" Gurmukhi script (Robert Montgomery, Judicial Commissioner).[7] Lurking in their dislike was their fear of the courageous Khalsa army created by Maharaja Ranjit Singh, and the political power of its "Goormukhee" script, for even after their victory in the Anglo-Sikh wars, the British felt insecure. In the words of Charles Napier, the army's commander-in-chief in India, "The Punjaub has been twice occupied but it is not conquered."[8] For the colonial state Punjabi language had the potential of reigniting Sikh political aspirations, and so it had to be put down. Urdu was instituted as the official language of the administration, with English dominating the upper tiers of power. A majority of Muslim intellectuals, journalists, and politicians gave up Punjabi and adopted Urdu, making it the symbol of their Muslim identity.

A counter movement was launched by the Hindus to replace Urdu. The Arya Samaj with its network of Dayanand Anglo-Vedic (DAV) schools and colleges imparted religious and secular instruction in the Hindi language with its Devnagari script, "a newly formed medium from Benares and Allahabad."[9] The Sikhs returned to their sacred language Punjabi in Gurmukhi characters, forging the triple Punjabi–Gurmukhi–Sikh equation. The Singh Sahbas started schools for the teaching of Punjabi, developed Gurmukhi fonts for printing, and generated a flurry of literary activity including the publication of numerous journals and newspapers in the Punjabi language. They tried to reach the villagers, create liaisons with Sikh regiments, and pressurized the British administration to introduce Gurmukhi in the Government school curriculum. In spite of their efforts, in the three-way conflict among Urdu, Hindi, and Punjabi, Punjabi lost out as Punjabi speaking Muslims opted for Urdu, and Punjabi speaking Hindus for Hindi.[10] At the independence of the subcontinent in 1947, Hindi became the *rashtriya bhasha* ("national language" in Sanskrit) of India, and Urdu the *qaumi zaban* ("national language" in Arabic-Persian) of Pakistan. On this divisive stage it is most admirable that a "Hindu" Dhani Ram and a "Muslim" Sharaf would ardently promote the language of a "Sikh" Bhai Vir Singh.

Bhai Vir Singh

Bhai Vir Singh attended the Church Mission School, read English writers and philosophers, absorbed Western ideas, and thus broke away from the constricting classical structures and tropes. Simultaneously, he learnt Persian, Urdu, and Sanskrit; he went back to his own Indian roots, to his legendary protagonists Heer and Ranjha, to his Sikh heritage, and to his mother tongue Punjabi. He adopted many different genres to awaken his community to their own past with fresh and innovative insights. However, it is in his poetry that his message comes out most effectively. He published several collections, including *Mere Sainyan Jio* (My Beloved), for which he won the Sahitya Akademy Award.[11]

In his first poem included in this anthology ("Desire for the Beloved"), Bhai Vir Singh affirms the power of love. He maps it on the rich literary Indian repertoire that includes the Hindu Bhakti expressions of love between Krishna and his cowmaids, as well as the Indo-Persian romances of Sassi and Punnu, Heer and Ranjha, Layla and Majnun. His concluding lines:

> *He arup! Eh tarap uho nahi*
> *Dhuron tusan jo lai?*
> *Ki eh chinag nahi oh jehari*
> *Tusan seenian pai?*
> *Milan tusanu di eh locha*
> *Eh hai tarap tusadi, –*
> *Jithe ramaz pave koi kattki*
> *Eh kamali ho jai!*

> Oh formless One! Isn't this the desire
>   You ignited at the beginning of time?
> Is this not the spark
>   You set in every heart?
> Our desire to meet you
>   Is our longing from you,–
> When your mystery strikes us
>   We become crazy for you!

His sentiments and diction loudly echo Bullhe Shah and Waris Shah. If in Bulleh Shah, Heer by calling for Ranjha becomes Ranjha herself ("Heer is Ranjha"), in Bhai Vir Singh, Leli crying for Majnun discovers that Majnun was but her ("Inner Blaze"). Like the Sufi poets, Bhai Vir Singh exalts love across religions; like them he unites physical and metaphysical love; like them he uses fire imagery; like them he traces its source to the divine One; and like them he admits that once struck by love, life transcends all neatly prescribed norms and takes on its own momentum.

Though fully aligned with the Sufi poets, Bhai Vir Singh's inspiration was his faith in Sikhism. Growing up in a devoted Sikh household, he naturally absorbed its expansive literary matrix. He made poety an integral medium for his hermeneutics, and succeeded remarkably in presenting the vision, the mood, and idiom of the Sikh Gurus. His poetry for instance is saturated with the personal pronoun *tun* (you) encountered in the Guru Granth. The vocabulary and metaphors and symbols for the Divine from the Sikh text – *agam* (unfathomable), *mali* (gardener), *rasa* (taste), and *nur* (light) recur frequently in his own poems. The title of his anthology *Mere Sainyan Jio* seems to be both based upon and in turn unfolding the scriptural verse, *"kar kirpa mere sain* – be gracious, my Beloved." Besides interpreting fundamental theological concepts, Bhai Vir Singh expresses essential Sikh moral and epistemological ideals as his poetic subjects existentially live them out. He is, to recall Emerson's analogy from "The Poet," a glass through which later generations can see the Guru Granth in its philosophical and aesthetic richness. Importantly, Bhai Vir also makes transparent that poets across religions share a fundamental affinity.

In his poem entitled "Golden Temple" the poet offers an aesthetic experience of entering the central Sikh shrine (in the city of Amritsar), the original Harmandar built by Guru Arjan to enshrine the anthology of sacred poetry. Without actually describing the rhythmic repetitions of intricate arabesques and latticework in gold and marble, or the mesmerizing way the shrine emerges out of the pool and reflects its beauty in its diaphanous waters, Bhai Vir Singh captures the sense of infinity generated by the space itself. He expresses its magic: just as you walk in, suffering transforms into joy. It is in his poetry that we discover Bhai Vir Singh's art at its zenith. Sometimes in his prose he is so intent on presenting the best of Sikhism, that he can be overbearing and pedantic. However, in short simple poems his deeply personal sentiments appear spontaneously, and like the Sufi poets, give us flashes of mystical intuition.

In "The Ruins of Avantipur," he comes across as a strong champion of imagery and visual art. Sikhism, like Islam, is an aniconic tradition, but the Sikh poet condemns religious fanatics who fear images and become victims of their phobias. His lament at the destruction of Hindu idols at Avantipur (in Kashmir) is a poignant reminder of the wreckage of the giant Buddhist statues in the Bamiyan Caves in northern Afghanistan by the Taliban shortly before 9/11. How could hatchets and explosives be employed to dismantle art that embodied such peace and serenity? What did the eyes see in these ancient images that they had to be destroyed with acts of sheer brutality? According to the poet, idols can be put back together from rubble, but the critical problem is the distorted vision: how do we begin *to see* reality? His poem ends with the desire for eyesight that will help people see through external differences and savor the intrinsic beauty of art belonging to humanity.

"Qutab di Lath" as he titles his poem on the Qutab Minar, is another important work that underscores the universality of art. The grand monument celebrating the victory of Islam on the Indian subcontinent was started by King Qutub-ud-din Aibak of the Slave dynasty in 1199 and was completed by his successor and son-in-law Iltutmish in 1230. Its fluted red sandstone is covered with intricate carvings and verses from the holy Qur'an in exquisite calligraphy. In this Islamic site also stands a much older iron pole with Sanskrit inscriptions. In fact the large Qutab Minar complex includes numerous pillars that are carved with indigenous Indian motifs, belonging once to Hindu and Jain temples. The poet begins by addressing the religious and racial origins of the monument that still stands in its glory in the Indian capital of Delhi. Does this creation belong to the Muslim emperor Qutub-ud-din who started its construction or does it go back to Prithviraj Chauhan, the Hindu emperor, defeated by the Muslims? Is it then from the Arabic or the Sanskrit world? Is it Semitic or Aryan in its genesis? As it rises to the climactic power of art, his lengthy rhetoric only goes to prove the futility of either-or categories. According to the poet, when the beauty of the monument is experienced, distinctions of religion, race, language, and creed dissolve: "*jati janam te asal nasal nun/ koi kade na chhane/jad sundarta darshan deve/ sabh koi apni jane* – Nobody cares for caste or birth/Or race or origins –/When beauty strikes,/Everybody adopts it as their own." The Qutab Minar belongs to the collective heritage of India, and its aesthetic joy is for all Indians alike. The poet values the monument's beauty as a force that burns up pride and prejudices, leaving the viewer with a renewed awareness.

The poet also describes many different facets of natural beauty. The area of Kashmir happens to be a palmful of boundless splendor – perfectly shot down from above! Bhai Vir Singh would visit Kashmir often, and each time carry its exciting jolt back home with him. His is not a romantic reverie. The poet creates a complex intimacy with nature. For instance, he compares Naseem Garden with a mother, but while a mother loves only her own children, the garden extends her comfort and love to every visitor equally. Nature is given a voice in his works, a serious voice in which human oppression and exploitation are forcefully criticized. The shy violet speaks, the chinar tree speaks, the kikkar tree speaks. In different tongues, the natural phenomena ignite respect and appreciation for the earth and her powers. Destined for the axe, the poor kikkar tree questions modern consumerism armed to destroy fields and jungles to set up its lucrative industries.

Throughout his poetry Bhai Vir Singh probes into the many complexities of the human psyche. The glimpses he offers into the innocence and pristine joy of childhood are delightful, and often bring to mind Rabindranath Tagore's images from his Nobel Prize winner *Gitanjali*. In "Struck by Desire" the poet opens up for us the garden of childhood where we discover a little girl playing dress-up with her dolls and pebbles with her friends. When she is sleeping her baby's sleep, the little girl has a dream in which a ring amidst dazzling moonlight is tenderly slipped on her finger. But her dream is full of other exciting "rings" as well, for words glittering in circles, spell out her beloved in a dazzling script. In an exquisite analogy from "Wild Berries," the almighty Lover is compared with a naughty child who not only snatches fig-candy from his mother's hand, but also takes enormous pleasure in eating each and every bite (*"khoh lae jiven khonda hai bal man de hatthon makhane/ te kha lae ikk ikk karke, suad la la ke"*). Bhai Vir Singh's childhood imagery stirs up a cosmic nostalgia; it takes his readers to the lost world of wonder and magic. By gathering the transcendent Infinite in the lap of a mother it unfolds images of the Divine that are generally neglected by society.[12] And *that* One relishing those wildberries reiterates the Sikh scriptural view of the wondrous beauty in *this* world of ours, giving primacy to the sense of taste spelt out in its epilogue.

Dhani Ram Chatrik

Whereas with Bhai Vir Singh we soar into ethereal realms, with Dhani Ram Chatrik, we are confronted with a powerful realism. He took his pen-name Chatrik from the bird which drinks only drops of rain, and therefore remains in a perpetual state of desire. He started his poetic career by recreating ancient Hindu romances of Damyanti and Radha from the Mahabharata and the Puranas. But soon he began to focus on contemporary social and political themes. Chatrik took up the shorter form conducive to presenting the barren landscape of the Punjab where, "There are no Heers left/Nor their sweethearts Ranjhas" ("Unemployment"), and the "waters of unity" are contaminated by fanatics ("O Wine-Pourer..."). In his poem "Whatever is Here," Chatrik puts many complex ideals squarely on the table including, "*mazhab hai ikk bahana* – religion is but an excuse." For the poet, then, *mazhab* (religion) has no intrinsic reality; it is merely a category for people to legitimize their actions and exploit the innocent. Loudly proclaiming, "Hell is but fear and heaven a false hope – *hai narak ikk darava te suarg hai ikk lara*," Chatrik urges his readers to attend to the social, political, and economic problems of daily life. Having lived through the tragic division of the Punjab in 1947, Chatrik fully understood how religion was manipulated by the elites to mobilize communal identity amongst the masses. In the name of religion two antithetical processes played out simultaneously: people were assimilated and included in their *own*, only to exclude and be separated from the *other*. In his simple language Chatrik tried to raise the awareness of his contemporaries so they could see themselves beyond their communalist ideology.

The importance of the Punjabi language is a vital theme in his works. Since language had become a marker of separate religious identity, Chatrik projects *her* as the mother who nurtured her children Hindu, Muslim, and Sikh alike. In his poem entitled "Three Mothers" (*Trai Mavan*) he places *her* along with goddess Laxmi and Mother Earth. By drawing upon the maternal matrix and reminding his readers that the language belongs to them, that it is their "life and breath," he motivates Punjabi people to treasure her. In his finale he even boasts, "*eho jehi manohar mitthi,/hor koi boli nahi ditthi* – So enchanting and sweet/ There is no language I see!"

Chatrik contributed to the Punjabi language in many important ways. Besides being a creative writer, he invented the printing font for the Gurmukhi script. By using modern techniques, he published the Guru Granth, and major Punjabi reference works like Bhai Kahn Singh's *Mahan*

Kosh. At the local and national levels, he worked hard to raise the status of the language. He was the founding president of Punjabi Sabha, a Punjabi literary society. Chatrik realized the powerful link between culture and language, and tried to change the consciousness of his people by communicating with them in their tongue and by urging them to take pride in the maternal *body* that gave them birth and fed them her life-giving nutrients.

He also returns to historical figures like Queen Nur Jahan (1577–1645) and Maharaja Ranjit Singh (1780–1839). For Chatrik it does not matter whether one is Muslim and the other Sikh, whether female or male, whether one is a migrant from Iran or a native of India; these two personalities for him are the markers of a pluralistic milieu in which people from different religions and races could live together as authentic subjects. It is admirable that rather than focusing on the great Mughal emperor Jahangir, our Punjabi poet recognizes Jahangir's wife Nur Jahan as the font of justice, tolerance, and harmony. Chatrik turns to her as a "sister" (*bhain*). His affectionate term becomes a metonymic marker for Nur Jahan's warm gestures and gifts commemorated by some historians. Indeed, she opened new avenues for inter-cultural understanding; she helped needy women irrespective of religion, class, or caste; she participated in Shia, Sunni, Sufi, and Hindu celebrations. Paintings from the Mughal era display the Muslim Queen playing Holi, the Hindu spring festival in which people smear and splash colors on one another. In art, architecture, embroidery, fabrics, Nur Jahan innovatively synthesized traditional Islamic abstract designs, representational forms from her Persian heritage, and the local imagery from the Indian context. Chatrik's designation "*bhain Punjab di*" (sister of the Punjab) especially evokes the magnificent caravanserai she built in the Jullundur district of the Punjab close to his own home in Amritsar. This Nur Sarai, where two thousand or more travelers with their horses and camels could stay at a time, would have played a highly important role in the political, economic, and cultural life of the Punjab. Its impressive gateway has the inscription acknowledging the "angel-like Nur Jahan Begum" as the founder of the Sarai, and its numerous panels display her brilliant aesthetic vision as stylized arabesques embrace paradisal trees, and typical Indian images of elephants and lotuses.

Interestingly, Bhai Vir Singh who like Chatrik belonged to Amritsar, also has a nostalgic poem on the Mughal Queen. In very tactile language a chinar tree speaks, "*pyar lain nun ji kar ave/ uchal kaleja khave:* We long to be

caressed/– Our hearts surge with desire." (The term *kaleja*, literally "liver",
is used here as the seat of love.) The chinars grow in Kashmir, that
exquisite piece of land "apart from the world," so adored by the poet.
Since it was Queen Nur Jahan who popularized Kashmir as a summer
resort, the tribute voiced by nature is most fitting. It is highly emotional as
well, for the chinar tree sorely misses the affection and tender touch of
Nur Jahan's hand! Both of our modern Punjabi poets express their deep
kinship with the historical person, and lyrically record her humanity. Their
alluring memories are diametrically opposed to the observations of agents
for the Dutch East India Company who judged ambitious imperialist
agendas behind Nur Jahan's artistic and charitable endowments.[13]

Chatrik yearns for the "sister of the Punjab" to bring back her era
when people from different religious and cultural backgrounds embraced
one another like siblings. Coming from the womb of Mother India, they
could freely sit together and remember the Divine in their own language:

> *Hindu Muslim ikk san*
> *ikko ma de lal*
> *japde ram rahim nun*
> *bahi ke nalonal*

> Hindus and Muslims were bonded together
> – They were sons of the same mother;
> They recited Ram and Rahim,
> Sitting next to each other.

He juxtaposes that wonderful pluralistic past to the twentieth century,
with its ghastly scenes in which those very Hindu and Muslim brothers
tore up their country along religious lines and mutilated each other.
"Truth," says Chatrik, "is so ashamed that it holds a handkerchief across
its face – *sach sharam da maria muhn te lae rumal.*" In this graphic image from
his poem on Nur Jahan, the poet says it all. In everyday life women have
to hide their faces because they should not be seen, but in this case, truth
is hiding itself so that it would not have to see the horrific reality.

In his poem on the Taj Mahal, Chatrik evokes another Mughal queen,
Mumtaz Mahal (1593–1631), for whose beauty and love her emperor
husband Shah Jahan constructed the famous mausoleum on the banks of
the river Jumna in Agra. Mumtaz was Nur Jahan's niece (her brother's
daughter), and the Taj Mahal itself bears an inherent relationship with the

artistic patterns of the exquisite mausoleum built by Nur Jahan for her
father Itimad-ud-Daulah in Agra. (It is nicknamed "Baby Taj" though in
fact it is the "mother" that gave birth to Shah Jahan's grand monument!)
However, the poet's communication with her is remarkably different.
Whereas he invites Nur Jahan to transform his brutal age into her glorious
era, he simply questions Mumtaz about her tensions and anxieties as she
lies in her eternal sleep next to her husband. In the latter's case, time past
is not ruptured from the present. The poet wants to know exactly how she
is feeling and thinking at that moment. His verse is not informed by any
philosophical theories or doctrines about life after death from any
religious worldview. Chatrik's questions are strikingly mundane – "how
does time pass for her? Do worries and fears disturb her here? Do her
eyes ever unconsciously open up?" And yet they are profoundly
disturbing. The monument memorialized as the "teardrop on the cheek of
time" by the Nobel laureate Tagore, functions in Chatrik's verse as a
marble mirror, which reflects human angst. In her silent response, the
sleeping Mumtaz Mahal acquires a surreal reality that startles the reader.
Death embraces a new mystery, and life itself acquires an existential
awareness.

The sentiments that Chatrik expressed for Nur Jahan emerge in his
tribute to the first Sikh Emperor Maharaja Ranjit Singh (1780–1839) at his
death centennial. Called the "Lion of the Punjab," Ranjit Singh built an
enormous empire in which the majority of the population was Hindu and
Muslim. Chatrik echoes historical memories of Ranjit Singh funding the
construction of mosques and temples, contributing the expensive silver
doors at the Temple of goddess Kali, paying an inordinately high price for
a manuscript copy of the holy Qur'an,[14] and patronizing festivals like Shah
Husain's 'urs, which notes Richard Wolf, became a major spring Sufi event
drawing Sikh, Hindu, and Christian pilgrims.[15] Chatrik extols the Maharaja
for his vision and accomplishment in uniting his religiously diverse people,
and even compares him with Bismarck. He praises him for his devotion to
his Gurus and for his contribution to Sikh art and architecture, including
the expensive and beautiful decoration at the modern Golden Temple.
Above all, Chatrik seems to admire the Maharaja for the special place he
occupied in the hearts of the people. It is the Maharaja's interior humanity
that matters most to the poet. And just as he does in the case of Nur
Jahan, Chatrik contrasts the glorious reign of the Maharaja with his own
decadent milieu:

> The country still is heavily populated:
> Mian, Lala, Sardar
> Inhabit it.
>
> Every home has a spark of grandeur,
> But alas, we do not see
> Any authentic Punjabi!

"Mian, Lala, and Sardar" are appellations of respect amongst the Muslims, Hindus, and Sikhs respectively. (Waris Shah repeatedly used "*mian*" in his invocation.) This poem written for Maharaja Ranjit Singh's death centennial offers a view of the situation in 1939: eight years prior to the Partition, the Punjabis are already turning divisive. The three communities happen to be living geographically close to each other in grand houses, but the poet reveals their moral paralysis. Chatrik's mnemonic strategy provokes his readers to assess their human potential; the "Punjabis" must regain the openness they once possessed.

Poetry for him is not for poetry's sake; it serves a crucial function. The citizen who yearned for social and political cohesiveness, took up writing poetry to fulfill his desire "to sew torn hearts – *pate seene sion lai*." His anthologies include *Chandan Vari* (Sandalwood Garden), *Kesar Kiari* (Saffron Flowerbed), *Nawan Jahan* (The New World), and *Sufi Khana* (Sufi House). Poetry was Chatrik's medium to transform the way people felt, thought, and lived. He concretized his goal by resurrecting historical figures, exploring natural rhythms, pointing out social behavior, and even idealizing marital harmony. The couple for him served as a microcosm for the larger social and political unity, and so if the husband and wife were united in their fundamental ideals, the macrocosmic family would too. He boldly declared religion as a mere pretext and disclosed colonialism, nepotism, unemployment, exploitation, and bigotry as the core of conflict domestic and national. His blatant critique of economic greed applies even to the 21st century global capitalist market in which multinational corporations are wreaking havoc on the underprivileged. Chatrik was immensely popular because his use of metaphor, tone, and style struck a deep chord among all Punjabis.

The way he weaves social and economic problems into childhood rhymes like the "*Kikkali Kali*" is tremendously effective. *Kikkali Kali* is a popular Punjabi folk song that accompanies a game played by girls. The girls get in pairs, plant their feet firmly across from each other's, and then tightly holding each other's crisscrossed hands, they go round and round, faster and faster, singing *kikkali kali* (something along the lines of our nursery rhyme *ring a ring o'roses*). But in this familiar childhood rhyme, the poet inserts a vehement criticism of exploitation, bribery, black markets, and society's reduction to slavery by the seduction of money markets. His litany on nepotism with "so and so related to so and so related to so and so" goes on and on. Long after we put down Dhani Ram Chatrik's work, the social maladies continue to spin in the psyche. It is unfortunate that the great poet is not properly remembered. Recent newspaper articles have reported about his house being in a state of shambles, and his children unable to read the Punjabi script, – which he fervently championed, and in which he brilliantly penned his deepest desires.

Firoz Din Sharaf

Likewise, Punjabis owe profound gratitude to Firoz Din Sharaf for his phenomenal contribution to their literary world. It was most courageous of him to be advancing Punjabi when his Muslim community was staunchly promoting Urdu. "I am a Punjabi, says Sharaf, I am devoted to Punjabi/I desire the success of Punjabi forever – *main punjabi, punjabi da sharaf sevak/sada ahir punjabi di mang da han*" (from his poem entitled "*Main Punjabi*"). In a period rife with religious conflict, Sharaf burrowed deep into the Punjabi soil, and experiencing its intrinsic pluralism, he projected it in powerful lyrics. To his contemporaries shackled in narrow provincialism, Sharaf showed a vast reality. The eminent Punjabi writer Dr. Mohan Singh recognizes his unique stance: "*uh na te kise ikk dharam de han, te na kise ikk sabhyata de* – he does not belong to any one religion, nor is he confined to any single culture."[16] After the Partition, Sharaf served as the Cabinet Minister of the Punjab in the newly created Pakistan.[17] On the Indian side, the Department of Languages in the Punjab published his collection of verse in two volumes (*Sharaf Racnavali*, 1972).

This fervent lover of Punjabi was born in a village near Amritsar.[18] Having lost his father soon after his birth, he succumbed to a life of penury. His family could not afford to send him to school, so he spent his time watching village magicians and snake charmers. Even though he was taken to the urbane Lahore as a child, the elemental village life that the toddler imbibed would later flow out exquisitely in his poetry. Sharaf is described to have been a dark complexioned, medium built figure, dressed in the typical Lahorie shirt and salwar, and invariably seen enjoying his betel nut (*pan*). Early on in life he started composing poetry in Punjabi and

Urdu, and by 1934 he had published numerous anthologies. He was also a regular contributor to magazines. He avidly participated in poetry symposia, winning many hearts and awards. Those who did not take Punjabi seriously as a literary language or thought that it lacked the poetic sophistication of Urdu, Sharaf proved them wrong with his mesmerizing recitations. Poetry became his sole means of financial support. Ironically, the fellow who barely made it through second grade deserves to be studied by scholars and critics for his literary finesse; the person who grew up in impoverished circumstances enriched the Punjabi language with the most precious gems.

In his autobiographical composition "I am Punjabi" (*Main Punjabi*) Sharaf acknowledges his multilingual background. He understands Persian, speaks fluent Urdu, he is familiar with English, but he reserves "love" (*piar rakhan*) for his "own language" (*boli apni nal*). He boldly refuses to take up Urdu in the land of the Punjab: "*ravan eithe te u.p. vich karan galan? Aisi aqal nun chikke te tangda han* – live here and speak the language of the United Provinces? What sort of stupidity is this?" Here inexplicitly, yet acutely, Sharaf condemns the colonial masters for imposing a language spoken in another region on the people of the Punjab. He revels in the free and passionate aesthetics of the classical poets: "*waris shah te bullhe de rang andar, dob dob ke jindagi rangda han* – I live my life fully dyed in the colors of Waris Shah and Bullhe." Language and reality do have a tight bond. Dyeing has been a very old and important profession in Islam, and Sharaf's trope draws upon the Muslim expertise in the chemistry of colors.[19] In turn for an east Punjabi reader like myself, it brings fond memories of "Masterji," one of the few Muslims left in the town of Patiala, whose craft of dyeing dupattas and turbans is revered all over postcolonial Punjab. His shop is a magical place smack in the bazaar with cauldrons of different colors, and no washing machine can ever fade any material once dipped in any one of them. Sharaf confidently presents himself steeped in the brilliant Punjabi colors of his literary predecessors that would never wash off – no matter how much the colonial officers or the intellectual elites tried to expunge.

Like Chatrik, Sharaf unabashedly proclaims the beauty and power of this language, and tenderly utilizes the maternal symbol. In "Homage" (*Arati*) he reminds his contemporaries of their "immutable bond" (*pakka nata*) with their Mother Punjabi (*punjabi mata*) at every stage of their life: she is the one who puts them to sleep with her lullabies, she is the one to marry them off with her wedding songs, and she is the one who accompanies them with her dirges to the world beyond. And much like Chatrik, he shames his audience for alienating their progenitor: "*pairan de vich gairan roli* – we have crushed her under our feet like a stranger." Sharaf's lovely consonance between *pairan* (feet) and *gairan* (strangers) is impossible to reproduce in English. He artistically divulges the obsession with linguistic partisanship that sundered Punjabis from their very being. Nevertheless, Sharaf's empathy for the Punjabi language resonates with hope: "*jag pae hun puttar tere/bhar devange khata* – your sons have now woken up/they will fill up your treasures."

An authentic Muslim, Sharaf extols the ten Sikh gurus, Sikh scripture, the creation of the Khalsa by Guru Gobind Singh in 1699, the rule of Maharaja Ranjit Singh, and the heroism of the Akali Sikhs in the independence movement. In Sharaf's lyrics, Sikh history and philosophy become palpably alive. In "Defeated" (*Hare*) the poet sketches several popular episodes of Guru Nanak's biography imprinted on the collective Sikh memory. (The tree stands still to provide shade to the sleeping Guru Nanak, the granary he worked in remained perpetually full in spite of him giving away generously to the poor, with his outstretched palm he stops a huge rock hurled at him, his shroud is left without the body and flowers are found instead so both Hindus and Muslims carry them away – to cremate or bury according to their respective customs.) But by admitting his own "defeat" to fully express Guru Nanak's grandeur, Sharaf keeps the reader's imagination reeling. He succeeds in reproducing the crucial feature of Guru Nanak's personality: "*hindu kahin sada, muslim kahin sada* – Hindus say he belongs to us; Muslims say he belongs to us..." In an elemental flow, Sharaf returns to the universal message of Guru Nanak and reinforces its pluralism for his contemporaries. Sensitive to language, the poet praises the Sikh Guru for his hermeneutic expertise: "You explain the terms from the Ved and the Qur'an better than all the Pandits and the Maulvis." Latent here is his critique of those elite theologians and scholars who were fomenting communalist ideologies amongst the Muslim, Hindu, and Sikh masses. In his large repertoire Sharaf zooms in on the distinctive qualities of the ten Sikh Gurus, and portrays each one of them with an oracular existentiality.

Sharaf also praises Bala and Mardana. In Sikh narratives and paintings we hear and see Guru Nanak frequently attended by a Hindu Bhai Bala, and almost always accompanied by Bhai Mardana, his Muslim rabab player. In Sharaf's text these popular devotees are endowed with their own subjectivity. They recognize the spiritual energy of Nanak and they feel its intensity. In the case of Mardana, the poet uses the ubiquitous Sufi symbol of a mystic lover as a moth attracted to the candle's flame and makes a delightful pun on his name. "Discerning the divine light of Nanak, Mardana came flying over and became intoxicated with his Name… In his love, he died over and over (*mar mar ke*) and so became Mardana." On the other hand, Bala is specifically inebriated by Guru Nanak's "intoxicated eyes" (*nain nasheele*). Again Sharaf evokes Sufi symbolism of intoxication: Nanak is so in love with the Divine that his individuality is annihilated (*fana*) and taken over completely by the Beloved (*baqa*). Guru Nanak's divine ecstasy is contagious. His externally "drunk" eyes show it all. Like Bala we too can see the infinite One by looking into the Guru's all-encompassing eyes that see beyond man-made divisions. Compositions such as "Mardana" and "Bala" reveal historical figures from different religious backgrounds in a dynamic relationship with the first Sikh Guru, and leave the reader with a mysterious radiation of his presence. Sharaf's use of Sufi aesthetics compounds the Sikh Guru's portrait.

Sharaf possessed a keen political awareness, and subtly drew attention to current events. His works capture the early twentieth-century struggle of the Akali Sikhs to retrieve their sacred shrines from the control of the decadent hereditary custodians (Mahants) – who went against Sikh principles but had the support of the British. In the "Martyrs of Nankana," Sharaf conveys the tragedy of 1921 when non-violent Sikhs suffered the calculated barbarity of the custodian at Nankana, the birthplace of Guru Nanak. He makes us taste the nectar that filled the young Sikhs with heroism, hear brutal gunshots, see innocent blood splash, touch tender bodies delicate like flowers, and smell their skin being lapped by the burning oil. Sharaf sensuously describes the scene when, as Mahatma Gandhi put it, the Mahant had "out-Dyered Dyer."[20] The British Brigadier-General Reginald Dyer had commanded his troops to open fire on the innocent Indians gathered at the Jallianwallah Bagh in Amritsar for the spring festivities of 1919. According to official estimates, nearly 400 civilians were killed, and another 1,200 were left wounded with no medical care. Sharaf recalls those atrocities too. Most important for the poet is the intimate bond shared across religions:

> *ikko rup andar ditha sarian ne*
> *uh rahim, kartar, bhagwan ethe*
> *hoe zamzam te ganga ikk than kathe*
> *ralia khun hindu musalman ethe*[21]

Everybody saw That One of the same form
Rahim, Kartar, or Bhagwan was no different from the other
The Zamzam and the Ganges joined at the same spot
The blood of the Hindu and the Muslim fused with one another.

As the waters of the Zamzam well from the holy city of Mecca join the sacred river Ganges flowing down Lord Shiva's tresses at the spot right next to the Harmandar, they inspire us to dream a new world. There is nothing artificial about Sharaf's style. Images and words flow out naturally, and hit the reader viscerally.

Also admirable is the male poet's sensitivity towards women. In "Broken Sitar" (*Tutti Sitar*) Sharaf tenderly depicts a voiceless woman discarded by her lover and ostracized by her society. She is a metonymic marker of the abandoned Punjabi language: once intimately close to her lover's vocal cords, her mesmerizing songs and powerful sounds reaching the skies above and the netherworlds below, she now sits in a corner, voiceless. The spectral "hand" that wrenched her from her lover alludes to the colonial machine with its invisible operations. "At Her Daughter's Grave" (*Dhi di Kabar te Ma*) we hear the poet empathizes with the agony of the mother who is still in the denial stage. The pain is intensified by the mother's guilt – for making her daughter do household chores, and the violation of propriety – how could she let her virgin daughter stay alone out in her grave! The tragic closure to her little daughter's life is conveyed through most ordinary scenes: her wardrobe is left unfastened, her window is wide open, her earrings and bracelets lie on shelves, her dolls and toys are spread out... Fraught with anticipation, Sharaf's scenes bring out the finality of death in a most heart-wrenching way.

For the poet the visible world is a part of the spiritual cosmos, and in several works he underscores their nexus. His poem "The Beloved's Hair" offers an inspiring understanding of *kes/kesha* (long hair), one of the five physical markers of Sikh identity.[22] It is a romantic piece on the beloved's wet hair as it caresses her beautiful face and lithe torso. Amongst his manifold descriptions the poet evokes spectacular terrestrial (slithering snakes) and celestial (touching the stars) images. The *kesha* unfolds divine mystery, for the poet is able to read "each word scripted in black ink." As in the case of his Sufi predecessors, physical love (*ishq-e majazi*) is the conduit for metaphysical love (*ishq-e haqiqi*). The finale of Sharaf's poem celebrates the erotic and spiritual synergy of *kesha* as they "transport us from the corporeal to the Divine door – *kharde majazi vicchon rabb de dware kes.*"

The poet possesses a strong practical streak, and a desire to reach the masses. These come out strikingly in poems like "Exercise" (*Warzish*). Here Sharaf reiterates his integrated view of the human being: with physical activity not only do limbs shine like gold, but Divine intuition and intelligence also begin to flow in the veins and arteries. Decades ago the poet was propagating that we take care of our physical selves so that we can be intellectually, emotionally, and spiritually fit. Many enthusiasts on their ellipticals and treadmills in the twenty-first century would share his wish to be exercising till the day they die. There is no mundane topic for Sharaf. His lyrics endow every bit of life with enchantment. His bouncy Punjabi rhythms and lively scenes keep dancing in the minds and on the tongues of his readers.

Now that the Punjabi language has become narrowly identified with the Sikhs, the contributions of writers like Chatrik and Sharaf acquire an ever-greater significance. They need to be duly acknowledged for the exceptional role they so courageously played for its advancement and success. They show us the way to move out of religious and national constructs. Their poetry heals the pain from conflicts both internal and external. These modern poets endorse the contemporary desire for "Punjabiyat" – "a transnational linguistic and cultural identity encompassing what are today Indian and Pakistani Punjabis and the global Punjabi diaspora."[23] Indeed, the lyrical writings of Bhai Vir Singh, Dhani Ram Chatrik, and Firoz Din Sharaf provide the mortar to build anew the shared cultural universe of all Punjabis.

Bhai Vir Singh

ॐ ❧

Desire for the Beloved

The cowgirls longing for Krishna
    That people speak of,
Sassi writhing for her Punnu
    That the desert sands record,
Heer's angst for Ranjha,
    Or Majnun's sickness –
These do not display love;
    These hide a deep mystery.
Oh formless One! Isn't this the desire
    You ignited at the beginning of time?
Is this not the spark
    You set in every heart?
Our desire to meet you
    Is our longing from you, –
When your mystery strikes us
    We become crazy for you!

The Chinar Tree from Ichabal
and Nur Jahan

Upon the touch of a beautiful lady –

Like you many have come
And stroked us softly,
We long to be caressed
– Our hearts surge with desire.
But your love and tenderness
Are not found in any hand,
O Nur Jahan your touch –
How lovingly you caressed us!

A Piece apart from the World

I spotted "goddess nature"
    In the skies above
From that beauteous horizon
    She was gifting away joys.
She playfully stretched out her hand
    Guess what all came into it:
Mountains, hills, plateaus,
    And lovely meadows in between
With waterfalls, streams, and lakes
    – Just like tiny oceans. There were
Soothing shades, delicious breezes,
    Woods like exquisite gardens,
Snow, rain, sunshine, and clouds,
    So many seasons, so many fruits…
This boundless beauty was held,
    In that single hand.
Standing aloft the skies,
    With her eyes on the earth,
She opened up her palm, and threw
    All of it down
    – A perfect shot.
The spot on our planet
    Where this handful landed
That is 'Kashmir'
    A piece apart from this world.

    It belongs to the earth,
        But has a celestial base;
    Dazzling with beauty,
    Its earthly joys, tastes, and scenes
    Make our hearts ache for the Divine.

Kikkar Tree

With my head held up high
    I face the skies,
I look up for the Divine
    I look nowhere else.
I seek no hut, no cottage,
    No city, village, palace, or mansion;
In rain, storm, snow, or sun
    I stay with my head uncovered.
I desire only warmth
    Wafting from the Divine;
I leased a mere palm of land
    I subsist and grow on it.
I bloom, I blossom, I give fruit,
    Without taking, I depart;
I die without making demands
    For house, food, or blankets.
I drink water from the rain
    I live on the breeze for food;
I have been a standing yogi
    For ages, and will be for many more.
I don't get in anybody's way
    I don't set off any troubles
I renounced everything
    Without accruing any merit.
Destined for me alas
    Is the axe, O' world.

Chrysanthemums Haven't Shown Up?

Question: Why are the terrace gardens
                    So desolate so barren this year?
                    Why haven't the chrysanthemums
                    Shown up as they do each year?

Answer: Our heavenly chrysanthemums
                    Had begun their journey
                    But the road-keeper Indra,
                    Stopped them on the way.
                    He sent threatening clouds
                    That blocked their roads;
                    He struck thunderous lightning
                    That frightened those tender buds.
                    From the bloated skies
                    Came torrential rains
                    They flooded the land
                    And swallowed our plants.

                    Our lovely chrysanthemums –
                    Indra drained them away.
                    Could it be he replanted them
                    In his own heavenly gardens?
                    For sure our chrysanthemums
                    Have not shown up this year.
                    Our gardens are so barren
                    Thanks to Indra, the god of rain.

The Shy Violet

May I ever remain hidden,
    As I lie low in the garden;
May no eyes touch me,
    As I hide behind hills.

I take the color of the sky
    Devoid of all pride,
Yes, begging for poverty,
    I enter this world.

I drink the celestial dew,
    I swallow the sun's rays;
With moonbeams as my friends,
    I play with the night.

Intoxicated by my scent,
    I am lost in my state;
Yes, in the day, I am shy,
    I can't even face a honeybee.

When the naughty breeze
    Comes and hugs me,
I don't move my neck,
    I don't utter a squeak.

Alas, even so I am split apart,
    By those who inflict partings;
My delicate fragrance,
    Can't ever be concealed.

My desire to hide
    And walk away unseen
Will never be fulfilled
    Despite my pleading.

Naseem Garden

Your shade is as soothing
    As our mothers were to us,
Your lap is as cool and loving,
    Your shadows as gripping!

A mother only loves her child,
    You love all of us;
Whoever comes to you,
    You lavish your love on them!

Spinning Top

Like a weevil on the floor
    I was trampled upon
I could not have felt more worthless
    Than any worm!
But it struck me: I too
    Beauty and light must be.

In that rapture I lost my self,
    And when I became conscious
    What did I see?
I had wings with jeweled patterns,
I was living amidst roses!

The Golden Temple

Like the pain of a shell at the loss of its pearl
    Like the grief of a mother at the loss of her son
When a lover feels the lack of divine elixir,
    Chaos occurs in every direction.

A broken string, the distressed, comes to your door,
    In rushes a wave changing the whole current;
What magic begins to play!
    Walls crumble, infinite bliss takes over.

Qutab Minar (Qutab Di Lath)

Are you Qutab, the creation of Qutub-ud-din?
    Semitic in your foundations?
Or are you *Pathar* [stone] the son of Prithviraj?
    So you'd be Aryan in your origins?
Or are you Qutab, the Pole Star?
    His younger brother?
While that Pole Star stays up in the skies,
    You are the Pole Star of our earth?

King Chandra had a pillar built
    Combining eight metals;
To keep his memory alive,
    The king installed it in this area.
Now tell me, did Prithviraj
    Have you built as his monument?
Are you a remnant of Hindu sovereignty?
    Which is no more?

Or like King Ashoka who sent his daughter
    To plant the seed of Buddhism in Sri Lanka,
Did Qutub-ud-din set you up
    As the symbol of Islam in India?
Or were you Hindu and
    Qutub-ud-din made you profess the *Kalma*?
You were first Hindu and then
    You entered into Islam?

Whoever constructed you, my brother,
    Made a grave mistake;
They did not leave any inscription
      Of their own name or place.
On the eight-metalled pillar
    "King Chadra" is inscribed;
By writing his name and identity,
    The ancient king made it clear.

Now had your ancestor
    Written down a word anywhere,
We'd be free from mind-boggling debates
    About your history.
You sound Muslim from Qutab,
    You sound Hindu from Lath;
But for us you are
    Our absolute Indian star.

Amongst the marvels of India
    You are a tower unparalleled
Whatever your race or pedigree,
    You are Indian.
No body cares for caste or birth
    Or race or origins –
When beauty strikes,
    Everybody adopts it as their own.

The Ruins of Avantipur

What is now left of Avantipur?
    Sheer skeletons of two temples!
These mute ruins from past civilization
    Speak of the cycle of time.

They bear witness to that eye
    Which had cataracts;
It was blind to beauty,
    It lost its virtue.

It could not discriminate
    Fanaticism from art;
Seeking to cure others, the iconoclasts
    Fell prey to their own sickness.

"Idol worship?" Statues were smashed.
    Art was lost.
Each broken idol can be easily repaired, but
    How do we create the sense of seeing?

Inner Blaze

Ablaze in love, crying, and searching
    The lover Majnun spent his entire life.

But Leli, his beloved, did not melt;
    She did not come to him.

At last Majnun gave up and sat still, with
    "Leli" "Leli" ever on his lips.

While he was devoted to his Leli
    Leli made her entry into his depths.

Leli too now ardently searching
    Came upon her Majnun.

"I am Leli," "I am Leli" she cried to
    Majnun who now was Leli.

The lover becomes the beloved
    When stillness abides within.

Our More Loving Beloved

Longing for his mother, the calf
    Broke his fetters and came to her;
The mother even more lovingly
    Licked and caressed him all over.

Longing for the ocean, the stream
    Crossed all dangers and finally reached;
The Beloved even more lovingly
    Rushed forward to welcome her.

Leaving Kashmir

When we part from beauty,
    The heart begins to sink;
But leaving you O Kashmir,
    I am not sad.

The exciting jolt
    You gave to my spirit
Inebriates me with joy –
    I am bringing it home with me.

Wild Berries

Wonderful are these tiny shrubs
    Growing on their own beside my hut!
Wonderful are their wild berries!
Wonderful are your marvels my Beloved!
Who knows you may come today
    Yes, refusing pears and apples
Yes, refusing a feast of apple berries
Refusing succulent berries as well
Round and plump and juicy and red
And all those shiny black berries
Yearning to be savored by you!
    Yes My Beloved, my handsome beloved!
You have arrived at my paltry home saying,
"I am hungry, I am hungry
Bring some wild berries growing beside your hut."

Trembling, quivering, rejoicing, but shy
    I picked some berries –
I was about to rinse them quickly, and
Place them on *arabi* leaves
In front of my Beloved
As my humble gift –
A gift that actually had been asked for.
But my Beloved rushed in
And snatched them while I was rinsing
– Like a child snatches fig-candy from the mother's hand!
My Beloved ate them all, one by one, relishing each berry
Wonderful my Beloved! Wonderful! I whirl in ecstasy!

Ah! Now
Listen to me my inward eye! I make one request:
Don't be rushed like these two eyes;
Oh please don't be in a hurry –
Treasure the image of my Lover forever.
    And you, my eyes,
    Let your tears flow,
    You deserve so.
    Your haste was the cause of our parting.

Henna

Last night my lover
　　Held me tight all night long!
His passion and his warmth
　　I am discerning today;
Visualizing these scenes,
　　I will rejoice forever.
Now tell me O friends, did my lover
　　Delight in touching me as well?

Waves of Love

On the night of the full moon
The ocean longs for the skies;
With beauty in the distance
Its waves surge in joy.
With the touch of the moonbeams
What does the ocean see?
A lover's heart, – which
Leaps like the waves.

Today

"Yesterday" is gone –
　　Far out of our control;
"Tomorrow" is still away,
　　Not yet in hand.
"Today" is with us,
　　Filled with worries though.
Caught up in yesterday and tomorrow,
　　We let today go for naught.

So hold on to "today" tightly –
Like ambrosial elixir, sip it slowly;
Absorb it, get high on it –
Immerse yourself in its divine radiance.

Rapture

A secret came from afar –
A wink from that ruler afar,
A flash from that throne above.
That secret raised my awareness,
This awareness took away my senses:
I dropped down dizzy,
I soared up high.
A delicate flutter took over,
Light splashed all over,
Fountains of life burst open –
Erupting euphoric tremors
Like vibrating notes
Rapturous, rapture they became.
O I went utterly insane,
Tremulous like waves.
If one were to ask,
What secrets could I divulge?
Melodious chords only vibrate,
Taut, they sing joyous tones;
A rhythmic form
Is like a braid tightly interlaced.
How to track the route of birds?
Mysterious are they rapt in rapture.

Struck by Desire

I was a little girl then,
    Playing dress-up with my dolls;
Playing games with my friends
    And singing songs with my brothers.
I was a little girl of tender age.

I was sound asleep locked in childhood sleep,
    Nobody was around me – no nurse, mother, father.
The moon in the skies was sending its silvery rays,
    Stars were emitting their caressing waves –
    Soft delicious waves hit my tender face.
You came cloaked in the night of silver
    You kissed my forehead in moonlight's dazzle,
You slipped a ring around my little finger
    Then bowing you whispered something in my ear.
I was sound asleep, but perhaps inside I was wide awake,
    You went away cloaked in the night of silver.

I woke up. I woke up from my baby's sleep,
    I looked around as though I were somebody other,
    Yes, I was a stranger to myself.
Wondering – was I lying lost somewhere?
    Or was I found and returning home?
    My young mind could not fathom.
My forehead throbbed in joy
    – A fountain burst inside –
    "What happened to my forehead?" I could not say.
My little finger shook, shooting tremors all the way,
    It had the ring I had received in my dream.
Looking around I saw words glittering in circles
    "Beloved! My beloved!" written in its dazzling script.
A constant melody echoed in my ears,
    It was the song "beloved! My beloved."
A naïve little girl I was struck by desire
    "Beloved mine, beloved, my beloved!"

You came back in a dream again,
    Flashing your effulgence you swept away,
– "It is me, me" you said in a musical symphony,
    But off you went not waiting a wink.
My desire grew even more when I woke up
    "Beloved, Beloved" I said, "please come to me"
"Close close, near me, here, closer to me
    Come my Beloved! Yes please do come for sure!
Kisses with your own lips see how they make it flutter
    My forehead, look at it, look also at my trembling finger –
    Yes, with the ring you slipped on, that too trembles;
It wants to touch your lotus feet,
Longing for a vision of your luminous form."

Dhani Ram Chatrik

℘ ଔ

Unemployment

Leave us alone love
    Enough of fleecing your fans!
Your music isn't enchanting,
    Your tunes are untimely.

There are no Heers left,
    Nor their sweetheart Ranjhas;
There are no more cattle,
    Nor prairies for them to graze.

There are no pitchers of butter,
    Or cowherds with curled mustaches;
There are no beauties whose curls
    Dance like snakes.

Our cheeks have lost their glow,
    Features show no life;
Bodies are limp, faces yellow,
    Eyes are huge, a vapid gaze.

Gone is the bounce of the deer,
    Gone is nourishing food;
There is no freedom, no happiness,
    There is no enticing youth.

How do we exalt you?
    Our hearts are heavy;
Misery weighs heavily
    Upon our empty stomachs.

Parents perish educating their young,
    Without employment in sight;
Life is spent in tears,
    Without any event to celebrate.

If in exchange for love,
    Employment could be gained,
You'd win thousands of devotees –
    Officials new and lively.

"No Vacancy" was the sign
    On each office I searched,
I spent the last penny
    On getting my shoes patched.

The wife says,
    "Sir, please get some flour from the bazaar."
Angrily he says,
    "Go away! Why do you devour me so O rascal?"

Unemployment has reduced
    Leonine youth to meek slaves;
For a tiny morsel, says Chatrik
    How many petty jobs I tried!

O Wine Pourer...

O Wine pourer! Quick! I beg you, please
Blend joys of life, make me a strong drink.
    Autumn has gone by, let spring shine forth:
    Awaken our sad slumbering hearts.
Break them – throw away our chains of bondage,
Free us – make us vigilant with your caress.
    O brave people of India! O shining youth,
    Create an army of devotees, solve her problems.
This is the motherland, our milk-giving cow, our heavenly home –
Greet her at her threshold with your head on your palm.
    Raise her flag high up into the skies,
    Make her future illustrious like the sun.
Laborer and farmer are the two arms of her body,
Bring her fame and glory on their strength.
    Make sure no one takes even a peek at her borders–
    At the slightest hint, like a roaring lion hunt them down.
You are the honor of your country; she, your honor,
So sacrifice unto her body and spirit, all your riches and possessions.
    India can lead the world with her guidance –
    Spread far and wide, her ideal of non-violence.
Hold truth as your support, and walk the path of goodness,
Lend a hand to the needy; generously pull up the downtrodden.
    Stay perceptive! Make humanity proud;
    Never give in to evil, always be moral.
Be compassionate: hear those in distress,
Expel the brutal rich; befriend the poor.
    If our country loses sight of high aims
    It is for you to get up and incite the low.
Black-market dealers, sly, greedy, bribe-takers –
Expose their base deeds, shame them in the marketplace.
    We have today midst us many mischievous aggressors
    Do not believe in their words whatsoever!
If fanatics contaminate the waters of unity,
Get rid of those idiots: show them their ignominy!
    Time is soon to usher in that perfect reign,
    O'Chatrik, try to wait a bit for that moment!

Our Language Is Punjabi

Our language is Punjabi –
Our life and breath
Our treasure of pearls
We won't let her go
Our language is Punjabi

In the melodies of the spinning-wheels
In the rhythms of the flute and song
We hear her full of beauty
Our language is Punjabi

In all our activities
In conflicts and wars
She is our life giver
Our language is Punjabi

Our bed of flowers
Our basket of joys
Never forget her
Our language is Punjabi

Life Partners

Life partners – with
Hearts united,
Same values, one goal –
Journey through life.

Two hearts must beat like one,
Like the two wheels of a train;
But if the destination differs,
They move – tentative, wobbly.

Nature's branch is auspicious
Man-woman a lovely couple, when
They aim high, keep their heads low;
They are more kind, less haughty.

Love, humility, virtue, service,
Truth, compassion, poverty –
May the couple with these seven,
Be blessed ever and ever.

Whatever Is Here

Cosmos is an intuition,
Life is a symbol.
Nature is a sport,
World is a vista.
Beauty is a lamp,
Love is a moth.
Earth is the motive,
Illusion is an expanse.
Existence is a gift,
Death is reality.
Life span is a flow,
And death is the shore.
Mukti is an ideal,
Religion is but an excuse.
Hell is only fear, and
Heaven a false hope.
Man is a traveler;
Hereafter, his destination.
Every journey is a tavern,
Desire its foundation.
Fortune is imagination,
Determination, the guide.
Destiny is a pretext,
Courage, a buoyant swing.
Humanity is a lush fig,
Its purpose, "public service."
Partnership is a blessing,
In the passage of the night.

Whatever is left of the night,
Let it pass joyfully:
I want to see the morning star
Ascending the skies.

Poet's Request to Queen Nur Jahan

You were the daughter of Iran,
    You were the wife of an Indian King
You were the sister of the Punjab
    For eighteen years.
Enter the history of the Punjab
    Our revered Queen!
If you do so,
    You will be remembered evermore.

During your time
    Unity prevailed in the Punjab;
Bring us that time again,
    Come and stand among us!
Hindus and Muslims were together
    – Sons of the same mother;
They recited Ram and Rahim,
    Sitting next to each other.

But this twentieth century
    Shows us horrible sights
Even truth is so ashamed that it
    Holds a handkerchief across its face.
Humanity is lost
    It is bleeding to death
The pages of history
    Have also hidden themselves.

Morality that triumphed high
    Lies beaten on the ground,
The seduction of gold
    Has reduced us to slaves.
Our spirit soaks in filth
    Our conscience is a corpse
Faith and Religion are beheaded –
    Severed by some sharp sword.

Three Mothers

My first Mother goddess Laxmi,
Created me and gave me wisdom;
For thirty-six years I have been
Studying and nurturing myself.
With her benevolence
I am in touch with good people;
God-willing, I will go to heaven.

My second Mother is India,
Whose soil gave me birth;
By devoting myself to her,
I have become a Punjabi poet.
I have spent my whole life
Imploring unity and harmony.
But now the milk has curdled:
Pakistan separated.

My third mother is Punjabi:
She brought me up as her child.
I clean and polish and wear and fix
Speaking and writing in its poetry and prose.
Casting aside the step mothers,
We enthrone her as the first wed queen;
So enchanting and sweet
There is no language I see!

Waves of the Heart

I came into this world
To spend a few days
In good company
And imbibe humanity, humility.

Perhaps as a means to earn my bread,
Or my interest in literature,
Or my desire to sew torn hearts,
I now write poetry for my country.

The Creator who is truly great
I have not been able to attain;
I can't intuit divine mysteries,
Nor explain them to the world.

Creed and communalism
Cannot seduce me;
My wings belong to the earth,
I don't make it to the skies.

I am not afraid of hell,
I do not wish for heaven;
I plead for humanity,
I will not exploit others.

All along I have exposed
God's cunning agents;
I don't want their loot
To prevail in the next world.

I am human – just like others –
Not a prophet, not a leader,
Not a saint, not a guru;
I don't want salvation yet.

A bubble on the sea
Can burst any day;
If anybody insults me,
I don't care.

A Desire

O Divine! With your blessing,
Just like my life has been –
Healthy and carefree
Full of laughter and glee
– May the rest be!

Whatever few days are left
May these bones and joints
Keep on moving smoothly.
Hope I don't have to
Ask others for help;
Give me the strength
To help others instead.

Flows the River

Down the mountains
Spinning in currents
Slapping against rocks
Flows the river

Stars strolling up above
Sparkle in its waves below
As it journeys along
Humming go go go go
Flows the river

Meeting with the sea
For the thousandth time
Up it soars in the heat
Only to return so
Flows the river

On the go – it doesn't stop
For the blink of an eye
Like a fountain controlled
Up and down over and over
Flows the river

Aspirations

When you have
The desire to choose
Your life's goal,

Feel free to be
King, ascetic, scholar,
Warrior or philanthropist;

But you must earn
Your living with the sweat
Of your own two hands.

Or, ask the Divine
To grant you devotion
Like the saints Tulsi and Mira.

The Song of the Rose

I offer honey to the bees
I adorn the beds of beauties
I attend on lovers as they stroll
I have the eyes of an eagle
I am a blooming rose flower

My face is bright pink
I grow tall quickly rooted
In the canopy that is Punjab
Waving over Mother India
I am a blooming rose flower

My aim is to rise up
To keep an eye on the world
To comfort the suffering
To do good deeds
I am a blooming rose flower

I support peace
I despise slavery
I desire the strength
To flush society's filth
I am a blooming rose flower

Freedom

For centuries we have been
Honing lovely dreams:
Wishing for peace and joy
Crying aloud our pain.

The fairy queen was
Upset with India; from afar
She witnessed our pain,
Our desperation,
                Our helplessness.

Thankfully the lovely dawn
With her flush of freedom –
Auspicious and full of joy –
Has arrived today.

The chains that bound us
For two centuries are broken;
The toil of Gandhi and Nehru
Has borne fruit at last.

I Found Out

Wearing your light grey scarf,
    You tried to hide away;
But its delicate lace
    Revealed your beautiful face.

The corner where you dwell,
    That is my meditation room;
I solved the ancient mystery:
    Your seat spreads through every heart.

Moth

From the moth, O rooster
    Learn the mystery of love:
It scorches in the flame,
    But does not utter a sigh.

"I am not a nightingale
    Who can sing her pain;
I am an insect,
    I sacrifice myself to love."

The moth dashes for the light
    Only to be struck down;
The flame extinguishes herself
    With the flow of tears.

Love is humanity's guardian, so
    Hold your emotions secretly;
They wane and fade
    When they are exposed.

Key to Living Happily

If you want a good night's sleep
    Stay away from the rich;
Better than being trapped by their treats
    Are scraps from the poor.

With bondage comes remorse
    Drying up the blood in us;
Our hands joined together, our heads bowed low,
    Lifeless we stand like a photograph.

Were a king to get a little angry
    His ministers could be hanged immediately,
When free from penalty
    Life in a hamlet is as happy as can be.

Why fill up with rich desserts
    When the heart is full of worries?
You can put on rags
    But make sure you live in freedom.

For Maharaja Ranjit Singh:
On His Death Centennial

I regard you as a treasure of wisdom;
    Caretaker of your kingdom,
    A general, a great hero.

You are the prime symbol of the Sikh kingdom –
    Devotee of the Gurus,
    Strong and generous.

You are the embellisher of the Golden Temple,
    You immersed yourself in your praise
    Of the plumed Master.

You dedicated your family to the Gurus,
    You set up shrines
    In their honor.

I honor your everlasting eminence,
    Your surveillance extended
    All the way to Multan.

Your leonine people roared your name,
    They sang your slogans
    As far as Kabul.

But my head is bowed low in respect,
    Because there was a spot for you
    In every heart.

You are the first prince of the Punjab
    Who valorously transformed
    The destiny of our country.

Each different spike you joined into a broom,
    You had the same vision
    As that of Bismarck.

If fate had not snatched you away from us,
    Our five rivers would be
    Far more glorious.

The country still is heavily populated:
    Mian, Lala, Sardar
    Inhabit it.

Every home has a spark of grandeur,
    But alas, we do not see
    Any authentic Punjabi!

With the passing of your bier,
    The map of the Punjab
    Tragically tore apart.

Only if you would return as our unifier,
    Our door to prosperity
    Would open wide.

Kikkali Kali

Kikkali kali
O girls *kikkali kali*
It was here just a second ago
O where did it go?
O the moment of freedom
Where did it go?
Who stole it?
We are left with this poison pill,
O the daughter of exploitation!
O the sister of black markets!

Now only that person is free
Who is totally oblivious to the Divine,
Who receives the sacrament of the bribe,
Who devours its each and every bite.

Here paternal uncle's son-in-law
Or maternal uncle's son-in-law
Or the wife's brother or the wife's sister's husband
Or the wife's sister's husband's sister's husband –
Each is minting money from his contracts
While we sit by the wayside.

Now everybody is a slave,
The world is enslaved to money;
Monetary markets lie wide open,
Everybody is obsessed with cash.

Slavery brewing
For two whole millennia,
Has seeped into the bones.
The slavery in the genes
Is robbing us from morning to night;
O the daughter of exploitation,
O the sister of deception.

O friends *kikkali kali*
O where did it go?
The moment of freedom
Where did disappear to?

Taj Mahal

White like moonlight's flower
Dazzling like a snowy crest
Lying on the crystalline breast of River Jumna
Moving to and fro – you embodiment of love!

Who was the artist who designed you?
Who was the king who financed you?

Your marble is like a mirror
Your texture softer than velvet
So dynamic are your patterns
    That our eyes can't rest
With you art comes to a stop.
Ancient, but you are so youthful;
For any dull heart, you are a flash of light.
The acme of the seven wonders of the world –
You are the crown of beautiful mausoleums.
You are the pride of India,
With you Agra is mapped as a pilgrimage site.

In your custody lie the treasures
Of the hearts of the Muslim kings.
Basking in her husband's love,
She lies asleep deep inside your walls.
What games of love does she play,
As she lies next to Shah Jahan?
Ask her, how does time pass for her?
Do worries and fears disturb her here?
Does she cherish his love?
Is she still inebriated as she was in this world?
Eyes full of bliss encircled by kohl,
Ready to strike, so proud of their beauty –
Do they ever unconsciously open up?
Seeing the spirit of her grieving husband,
Her sleeping spirit must surely awaken!
Their delightful experience of union
No longer plays out here.
Meeting and parting are part of life,
The rounds of destiny come and go;
But the flowers of passion bloom forever.

Waterfall

Glaciers melting on lofty peaks,
    Leave their homes far back, O friend!
Down come the waters,
    Beating and rumbling aloud, O friend!
With their force of faith, they fly and they flow –
    A waterfall they make, O friend!
A wonderful waterfall! Lovely friend!
    Your beauty is infinite, O friend!
Crystalline complexion, brilliant shine,
    A hint of azure blue, you have O friend!
Every pore beams with light,
    Your brilliance is so delightful, O friend!
Tender is your heart,
    You are most delicate, O friend!
Your cool touch, your lovely vista, –
    You soothe my mind and body, O friend!
To you who glide along the river of love,
    We sacrifice our life, O friend!
Following the flow of time,
    Your beat is ever rhythmic, O friend!
Your beckoning wafts bring birds
    To linger by your side, O friend!
Like thundering clouds
    You set melodies of Malar in motion, O friend!
Your movements we cannot see –
    You take away our senses, O friend!
Your seething passions froth and foam
    As they strike on rocks, O friend!
Your relentless beatings make obeisance –
    Searching for salvation, O friend!
You inspire all lovers, and
    You rejoice in their joy, O friend!
We find peace beside you, and
    We enter our Beloved's realm, O friend!
Such is our union, we never separate;
    We are one forever, my friend!

Firoz Din Sharaf

ဆ ભ

I Am Punjabi

I am Punjabi, an inhabitant of the Punjab,
    I am a villager and quite urbane.

I understand Persian, am fluent in Urdu,
    I know some English as well.

I am never embarrassed to admit
    That I love my language –

A pearl in a bride's nose-ring,
    A gem in a Punjabi woman's bracelet.

It has always been my desire that
    Punjabi be respected everywhere.

My life is vibrantly soaked
    In the colors of Waris Shah and Bullhe.

I'd live here and speak the language of U.P.?
    What sort of stupidity is it?

I am a Punjabi, 'Sharaf' a devotee of the Punjab,
    I wish the success of Punjabi forever.

Homage

Praise to you Mother Punjabi!
May fortune worship your feet!

Your lullabies are the games we play
Your songs are our wedding rites
Your dirges take us away from earth

What a strong bond there is!
Praise to you Mother Punjabi!

You are our melody
Every word, sweet as candy
But like a stranger we trampled you

We did not treasure you!
Praise to you Mother Punjabi!

Darkness has receded
For those who own you
Your sons have now awoken

They will balance your ledgers!
Praise to you Mother Punjabi!

A queen, you sit on a throne
You are the mistress of your home
'Sharaf' rejoices in your arms

May you have all the comforts!
Praise to you Mother Punjabi!

Defeated

How do I express my praise for you Baba [Nanak]
When so many have already tried in vain?

All the worlds have failed to find,
An alphabet to write your pure name in.

The light of your beautiful meditation,
Surpasses that of all the moons and planets.

The shade of your tree does not budge,
However hard the sun and its rays may try.

The guruship that you sprouted,
No land nor landlord could ever match.

Your instruction of terms from Veda and Qur'an,
Outshines the arguments of Pandits and Maulvis.

Your granaries constantly remained full to the brim,
Though accountants registered you giving stock away.

Hearing your word of the Divine One,
Countless demons like Kauda were defeated.

Seeing the line of fortune on your forehead,
Even inexorable destiny accepted defeat.

Seeing your grindstone move on its own,
Mighty Emperors like Babur were taken aback.

Seeing your treasures of spiritual name,
Notorious robbers like Sajan gave up their illicit ways.

Melting a stone-hearted Vali Kandhari,
Your power defeated the proud and arrogant.

Hearing your profound discourse from Bala,
Prodigious intellectuals lost their thoughts.

Such is the string you tied Mardana with –
Neither does it cease moving, nor does he.

The ocean of your verse is far too deep,
Countless scholars dived in only to drown.

Taking off to rob your infinite wealth
Many a criminal lost his way.

Seers and deities were left astounded,
By the game you played at the end Baba.

Hindus said he is ours, Muslims said he is ours,
But you magically slipped across!

You handed them the hem of your shroud,
And they started their loud disputes.

Says Sharaf, you have triumphed Baba,
They may keep fighting who knows till when!

At Her Daughter's Grave

Wake up O' asleep one! I sacrifice myself to you,
Your mother today has come to see you.

Look how the day has risen so high,
Your nocturnal sleep has still not withdrawn.

A maid in your attendance I come to wake you,
Get up and see how much I treasure you.

Open your eyes, see my little princess,
How your window awaits your appearance.

Go lock it up, walk over with me;
My daughter, your wardrobe is still wide open.

O pretty one, take care of your dolls – put them away
I cannot gather the game you had started to play.

The flower of my heart is woven like lace,
Each time I see your basket I writhe in pain.

When your friends weep for you,
Your poor needle has to cover its eye.

Was this shroud your dowry, my child?
We do not like its gold and pearl border.

Your comb inlaid with mirrors and gems,
Pierces our hearts like a sharp dagger.

Your flower-like face, your cypress-like height,
Your colorful scarf, – we see on every leaf.

How quickly your life closed up its shop,
With your bangles and earrings still on the shelves.

So many outfits you'd change during the day,
How could you fall for merely one now?

We were of course preparing for your marriage,
Even your doll is ready – all decked up in jewels.

You once brought life to this concrete building;
Your empty home now echoes like a tambourine.

With a beautiful neck like a pigeon
You flew away leaving us terribly alone.

You could barely carry one flower,
How do you carry these tons of clay?

O moon faced one, how do you pass
This dark night with the frowning stars?

Dead snakes seduce like their charmers,
How come nobody braided your open hair?

If you were ever upset, I'd try to cheer you,
Who'd be catering to your moods over there?

If it is housework that bothers you, my efficient one,
Don't worry: I'll do your cleaning and wash up.

Come love, let's go home. You are a virgin;
It is not proper to stay alone in a strange land.

If you don't come home with me, my daughter,
Your wretched mother will have to stay with you!

Mardana

At the flash of the divine light,
The moth came flying over;
Drinking the name of Nanak,
He was inebriated.
People thought he was drunk,
But he was gone far beyond;
Sharaf, he died in the name of love,
And so Mardana he was born.

Bala

As the divine light appeared,
Thick darkness receded within.
Seeing the Guru's intoxicated eyes,
He was inebriated.
On the rosary of his mind,
He turns the beads day and night.
Sharaf, for his devotion to the Guru,
Bala is known across the world.

Exercise

By exercising we maintain our health
By exercising we refine the beauty of life
By exercising we keep ourselves happy
By exercising we strengthen our humanity.

With exercise every disease disappears
With exercise the elder grow young
With exercise sloth keeps away
With exercise energy finds its way.

Limbs shine like bright gold
Cheeks blush with godly glow
Divine intuition and intelligence
Flow in each and every vein.

For a face shining like the risen moon,
Everybody is ready to sacrifice themselves.
A body like an arrow,
Won't ever turn into a bow.

Enemies get jealous,
Friends proudly rejoice;
In spite of old age,
Flexibility prevails.

There is no depression,
Only robust action;
Digestion and lungs improve,
Humans transform into iron....

How can I list all its virtues?
Or, its countless advantages?
May we exercise until
The day we die, Sharaf.

The Beloved's Hair

Black serpents began to swim
When she unfurled her hair;
Smitten by their fangs,
Waves started to blister.

Rare pearls were cast
When she squeezed them dry;
Tresses caressed her lithe figure
As the blush on a lover's face.

When she spread them out
The moon appeared in the clouds;
Gliding through the comb
They pierced many a heart.

Out of the comb and into the curls
Like poor me, they went in circles;
In the sparkling mirrors I read
Each word scripted in black ink.

Slick and smooth they shine
Like eyes lined with kohl;
As if measuring her height
They got tied into a braid.

Around an ivory face
The black snakes slithered and hissed;
The sequins bordering her scarf
Reached out to touch the stars.

Like snakes swinging in the gentle breeze
They swayed back and forth her slender neck;
The black curly beautiful hair
Day and night they lie on her breast.

A ladder of spiritual love, they transport us,
O'Sharaf, from the corporeal to the Divine door.

Divine Hues

Today your unfathomable eyes betray
Their seduction by the sight of another;
That is why they smile as I weep
Belonging to the cruel and merciless you!

Having stolen my heart down they gaze,
Like a thief they won't look up straight.
Smitten by your beautiful face I gaze,
Like a forlorn *chakor*-bird at the distant moon!

A fool I may be but my eyes are honed –
They detect every nuance of beauty
Just like the eyes on a peacock's tiny feather
See through the myriad hues of the Divine, Sharaf!

Victors

From your plume our beloved Tenth Guru [Gobind],
The pearl asked for its sheen, the rose its fragrance;
The lightning and the sun, their brilliance,
The moon, the stars, and the lamps, their glow.

Intellect, wisdom, faith, knowledge devotion, –
Each received its clue to the divine Truth they sought.
Some wanted property, some cattle and sons
Some asked for wealth and honor.

You happily gave everybody,
What each wished for, O' Guru.
But they profited the most,
Those who desired a glimpse of you!

The Martyrs of Nankana

Devotees of the Divine,
    Lovers of the Guru,
Sparkle of the eyes,
    What mysteries they unraveled!
When the group of Sikhs arrived here
    On behalf of their community,
Alas, how can I describe,
    The shots fired at them!
With each sip of *amrit*
    They had pledged their lives,
They now greeted the bullets
    With their arms wide-open.
Together, a procession of pilgrims,
    They came to defend their faith;
In the color of unity
    Their shirts got drenched.
Their blood squirted on one another
    Midst crackling sound of fire,
Gokula-Mathura trembled
    Ancient cowherdesses invited:
"Come out Lord Krishna
    Come and see this game too –
The ritual of *holi* being played
    With crimson blood."
Locking doors from the outside,
    The enemy set oil on fire inside;
The skies shook above,
    The earth quaked below.
With their feelings trapped,
    Their delicate bodies
Tender like flowers,
    Vanished in the inferno.
On the scales of devotion,
    With the weights of faith
They placed their lives
    Serving as a measure for all others.

The Broken Sitar

That's enough dear musician,
    Don't please touch me;
My wounds are still fresh,
    Don't fan their pain.

What attracts you
    To this form of mine?
What do you want
    From this ruined store?

Don't look at my flowers
    Engraved in colors,
I am a beaten block of wood
    Standing in a corner.

I was once robust too –
    With the bounty of spring;
I was soaring above
    Held up by love.

On my lips were bursting
    Songs of delicious truth;
On my breast were dancing
    My lover's hands.

The world would sway
    In the ecstasy of my song,
My lover too
    Would be inebriated.

My voice crescendoed
    To the peaks of the skies
The stones down below
    Melted into drops of water.

My lover and I
　　Formed a single note
I was with my lover
　　My lover was with me.

Streams of joy
　　Flooded the air,
As I'd sit in his lap
　　Embracing him tight.

But some hand struck,
　　And my strings broke;
I was wrenched from his neck,
　　Thrown away by my lover.

My shattered self,
　　He did not gather;
He took in his lap,
　　Somebody better.

Sharaf, she says, don't touch me,
　　I am voiceless;
O musician! I am not an instrument;
　　　　I am an abandoned woman.

Celestial Divali

In the pristine waters of the Harmandar
The stars are so enjoying themselves

Holding each other all tightly
As though they are somersaulting

Their fiery hearts are soothed
As they do cartwheels in the waters

To take refuge at the Guru's feet
These victims have come from far away

Lovers of the Divine are pouring
Their precious actions into Amritsar

Bright garlands of true love these
Rare diamonds sparkle magically

Traders of the Sovereign have offered
Their heavenly sons at the Guru's feet

These sparks of immutable love
Are crushed by gurdwara officials

Like bubbles against the wind
They hide in the pond's niche

Stars from the skies have sent
Lustrous balls for the fish to play

These twinkling boats have all
Pledged their ardent devotion

Their heavenly eyes peek – not from waters
But from a wall bedecked with mirrors

Those who will rain down light at dawn
Raise their heads like surging fountains

This bazaar of precious gems displays
The adorned eyes of the queen of night

When the veil of water slips off their face
How the butchers wreak havoc!

No, no, says Sharaf, this is Divali
Lighted up in the Harmandar by the stars

The Beautiful Punjab

Amongst beautiful lands
Amongst beautiful lands
It is the Punjab O'friends. It is the Punjab.

Amongst the flowers
Amongst the flowers
It is the rose O'friends. It is the rose.

Girls swing together in the gardens
Like lush vines,
Their fiery youth blazes high
   Jewels sparkle around their necks,
Decked in diamonds and pearls,
   Their faces are the moon, O'friends.

Amongst beautiful lands
Amongst beautiful lands
It is the Punjab O'friends. It is the Punjab.

Together they sit to spin
   And whirl away their spinning wheels,
Opening up their delicate arms
   They draw in thin strong thread.

They set hearts on fire! They set hearts on fire!
   Their lips are red jujube, O'friends!
Their lips are red jujube!

Among all beautiful lands, Punjab is the most beautiful O'friends!

Heer like a princess lies in her boat,
While her friends hop and play;
The stars sparkle around the moon,
   The friends, around their Heer.

Can't bear her brilliance, O'friends!
None can bear Heer's brilliance!
Among all beautiful lands, Punjab is the most beautiful O friends!

Here beautiful rivers happily flow
    Fruits and flowers abundantly grow
The Punjabis walk on their land
    Sharaf, with joy and honor.
        Sutlej, Ravi, Jhelum,
        Sutlej, Ravi, Jhelum
Attock and Chenab O'friends! Attock and Chenab!
        Amongst beautiful lands
        Amongst beautiful lands
It is the Punjab O' friends. It is the Punjab.

4

POSTMODERN FEMALE POET

In 1947 "the most beautiful land" lauded by Firoz Din Sharaf turned blue with poison and had to be amputated: its *western* limb was given to Pakistan; its *eastern* was left for India. As Lord Mountbatten, the last Viceroy of British India acknowledged, Britain granted independence not to one nation, but to two, and the Viceroy presided at twin independence ceremonies. The line dividing the two nations was hastily drawn by the British judge Cyril Radcliffe, who had never been to India. At the dawn of independence, the Muslim population migrated to West Punjab, which was allotted to the new nation of Pakistan with a distinct Muslim identity. Likewise, Sikhs and Hindus from the Western part were forced to cross over to the East Punjab, which now formed a part of free and secular India. During that mass migration of over twelve million people, internecine massacres became rampant. People on both sides of the Border were seized by a mad communal frenzy. Women were particular targets of sexual savagery on both sides. Trainloads of men and women migrants were horribly slaughtered, their bodies disfigured. No one knows the exact number for the huge loss of life. It is one of the gravest tragedies in human history.

Poets like Firoz Din Sharaf, Amrita Pritam, Mohan Singh, Prabhjot Kaur, Gopal Singh Dardi, Dr. Fakir Muhammad Fakir, Shiv Kumar Batalvi, Surjit Patar, Amarjit Chandan and others have been bringing in a message of hope. Their works remind Sikhs, Hindus, and Muslims of their common literary inheritance. These poets frequently return to the waters they drank from together, the fields they harvested together, the land they danced in together. In her *Ode to Waris Shah*, Amrita Pritam exhorts Waris Shah to emerge from his grave and respond to the tragedy befallen countless "Heers" in a war torn Punjab:

Today I ask Waris Shah to speak from his grave!
And turn to the next page of his book of love.
You saw one Punjabi daughter weep, you wrote page after page,
Today countless daughters weep, they cry out to you Waris Shah:
>   Rise! O sympathizer of the afflicted! Rise!
>   Look at your Punjab!
>   The land is sheeted with corpses, the Chenab is full of blood.

In a similar vein, her famous contemporary male poet Mohan Singh
returns to the idyllic Punjab where Muslims and Hindus and Sikhs freely
interacted. At a time when Sikhs and Muslims were dismembering each
other's bodies, psyches, homes, fields, and shrines, Mohan Singh
remembers the landscape of love immortalized by Bullhe Shah and Waris
Shah. A Sikh, he wants his ashes immersed in the River Chenab because it
is suffused with the spirit of the Punjabi Muslim heroines Heer and Sohni:

>   The spirit of Heer and Sohni
>   Flow with the Chenab,
>   Their feet walk its currents,
>   So immerse my ashes in the Chenab!

Without being carried away by the nationalism of India or that of the
newly created Pakistan, the poets speak to Punjabis on both sides of the
Border. They write in their common mother tongue Punjabi and use
common metaphors and rhythms that they suckled with their mother's
milk. Their works show that it was not religious or ethnic differences but
the divide and rule policies of colonial forces that caused their horrific
rupture.

Amrita Pritam poignantly remembers the literary giants of Punjabi
language and literature. In fact she offers a profound elegy for Dhani Ram
Chatrik. The despair and loss at the great poet's death is "a night which no
day follows" ("*Chatrik*"). Amrita honors him for creating "a shrine of true
art – *sachi kala di ikk dargah*." A Sufi site shared by Muslims, Hindus, and
Sikhs, "*dargah*" is the perfect expression for Chatrik's ingenious
accomplishments. True art has no boundaries; with its inherent force it
reaches out to everybody alike.

Pritam is the most prominent poetic voice of the new social and
political movement that emerged in postcolonial India. The 1935
International Conference of Progressive Writers in Paris was followed up

in Lucknow under the chairmanship of the famous Hindi writer Munshi Prem Chand. It brought in a new intellectual wave. Overall, the nationalist movement for the independence of India, the contact with Western ideas of democracy and freedom, the rapidly shifting realities of World War II, and the tragic division of the Punjab, intensified the social and political consciousness. In a progressive spirit, Punjabi poets broke away from the traditional past; instead of retelling the old legends, they enthusiastically embraced new modes and themes. "Motherland" and "Mother tongue" acquired a new immediacy and relationship, and contemporary public affairs mandated utmost urgency. Some of these poets were particularly influenced by the ideas of Freud, Marx, and Chekhov. Many started to pursue their social aspirations with a vehement intellectual consciousness, and Pritam became the most dominant figure of Punjabi poetry. She even saw through the progress of modernity, and in a postmodern spirit began to question the structures and simple binary oppositions that differentiate social progress from reversion, honor from disgrace, presence from absence, human from nature, male from female, West Punjab from East Punjab.

She was born in 1919 to a Sikh family in Gujranwala, which was subsequently allotted to Pakistan. Her father was a poet, and her mother a teacher. But Amrita lost her mother when she was only eleven. Perhaps she tried to fill in that maternal void by writing poetry, for she published her first anthology in her teens. Over the years, she took up different genres. Her feminist spirit emerges in all her writing, but it is in her poetry that we find its most subtle and boldly sensuous articulation. In her *Ode to Waris Shah* (above) we heard the painful beat of her saddened heart. She brings attention to the fact that the land of the five rivers and the land of the sons (heard in the verse of the male poets) is the land of daughters as well. Pritam speaks for all those women who were brutally silenced.[1] In many of her poems she powerfully protests the violence against Muslim, Sikh, and Hindu women – victims of abduction, rape and carnage during the fateful events of 1947. Not only do we see their dismembered bodies covering the land, their blood dyeing the rivers red at that moment in history, but we are also forced to examine the perpetuation of that horrific cruelty into the succeeding generations. Pritam's poem "Helpless" ends with:

Who would know
How difficult it is
To bear flagrant violence?
For a womb to carry life?
For limbs to burn, for bones to char?
I am a fruit of that time
When the berries of independence
Were beginning to sprout.
My mother's womb was helpless

Pritam radically criticizes the assumptions and structures of her modern socio-political world.

With a postmodern skepticism, she further discloses the violation of the female body where it would be least expected – amidst the beauty and grandeur of religious space. In temples across India females worship deities, and they are worshipped reverently as deities. The poet in her anguished voice expresses both these phenomena as sexist and misogynistic.

In "*Devata*" ("God"), for example, she portrays tall sinuous young women prostrating themselves before the cold, rock-hard physique of the male deity. The male gazes at his devotees and seems to derive a sadistic pleasure from the sensual and innocent young women passionately kissing his feet and caressing his limbs. In amazing detail the scenes in this short poem bring out the contrast between the power of the icy male and the subjugation of the fervent females. Towards the end of the text, the poet acknowledges that she too is a participant in his worship; but rather than being a human subject, she sees herself as an object smoldering in the oblation. For her reader though, the poet rises like a blazing flame – a courageous victor, who in her fiery diction reverses conventional notions of purity and pollution.

Kinian ku talian di chhoh
Tere pairan utte jamin?
Kinen ku hothan de ras
Tere charnan utte sukke?
Hare sajjan asin hare!
Pathar de juthe pairan nun
Mere pujan bhav kanvare...

How many palms have left
Their touch on your feet?
How many kisses from lips
Have congealed at your feet?
We have failed O good friend,
    We accept our defeat!
My pure virgin desires worship
Your polluted marble feet...

Like other poets in this anthology, Pritam poignantly criticizes formal religious rituals that repress the human spirit.

In another poem entitled *"Kanya Kumari"* she transports her readers to the actual temple of the virgin goddess on the southern tip of the Indian peninsula where the Arabian Sea, the Indian Ocean, and the Bay of Bengal flow into one another. Instead of the male (as in "God"/*Devata*) here the female (*Kanya Kumari*) is popularly worshipped. The terms *kanya* (virgin) and *kumari* (young woman) appear frequently in Pritam's work. Originally from Sanskrit, they refer to the aspect of female sexuality that has not yet quite ripened and is full of potentiality. They evoke the physiological and psychological complications of virginal sexuality permeating Pritam's discourse. She even prefaces her poem with the mythic account of Kanya Kumari: the young goddess is decked up in her bridal outfit, ready to get married to her lord Shiva. But the deceptive crows caw; the groom turns back thinking that the auspicious time of marriage has elapsed. The marriage does not solemnize, and the ritual rice grains slip from the distraught bride's hands.

Yet she still stands on the southern tip of India – still a virgin in stone, her auspicious rice also turned into stone. Devotees extol the virgin goddess as she stands in her fineries. Male and female pilgrims throng from all parts of India, and far away from diasporic communities, to pay their homage to this virgin goddess. They come to her to seek her blessings for marriage, prosperity, and the birth of sons.

Pritam's literary camera unveils the covert disparagement and subjugation that lies behind such overt celebration of the goddess. How would the goddess who was never married fulfill the marriage wishes of her devotees? In her unconventional approach it is the goddess in her miserable state who empathizes with the millions of flesh and blood virgins: *"iss dharti dian lakh dhian/main na ikk kumari/ishq samein da pathar hoia/pathar ho gai nari* – Earth has millions of daughters:/I am not the only virgin;/Love turned to stone long ago,/Women are stone."

Clearly the goddess is not an image of empowerment but a disappointed female reduced into stone by her androcentric society. The love that should have blazed is petrified in her case. Shiva rejects her, but in spite of his rejection, Kanya Kumari dedicates her life entirely to him. Such one-sided dedication must reduce any living person into lifeless stone. The imagery and symbolism of the *virgin* goddess send strong psychological messages to the young female worshippers that their most natural and creative female processes are impure and dangerous. Like the divine paradigm, Kanya Kumari, they too must serve their husband with their physical and spiritual might – despite the fact that the husbands (like Shiva) may turn their back against them. Pritam's poetry palpitates with the blatant truth that putting women on pedestals and worshipping them is the flip side of degrading and dehumanizing them – turning them into stones. This poem *"Kanya Kumari"* is a bold reminder of the Nepalese phenomenon of the Kanyadevi, in which a four to five-year-old girl (*kanya*) is chosen as *devi* (goddess), and is honored as a living goddess. She is lavished the highest spiritual and secular splendor – until the commencement of her menstrual period. She is then immediately returned to her parents, and ostracized for the rest of her life. Sometimes she cannot even marry because she is deemed inauspicious, a harbinger of danger and misfortune. Such intense honor and dishonor for the female body is terribly difficult to reconcile.

Pritam's feminist lenses keep digging deeper into the layers of sexism. In the poem entitled "Gift of the Virgin" (*Kanya Dan*) she unmasks the tragic reality behind wedding customs that continue to be vitally important in modern India. The gift (*dan*) *of* and *to* and *for* the virgin daughter (*kanya*) encompassed by her title *"Kanya Dan,"* is prized in every Indian home. It all sounds very positive and generous, but in the social fabric, the gifts and gifting prove to be intolerable obligations. Allied with "material" gifts, the daughter is viewed as an economic liability for her family. Skillfully utilizing funeral imagery, Pritam exposes festive marriage scenes as processes of manipulation and exploitation. The bridal henna designs are blotched, the sari the bride wears is more of a shroud, and the expensive jewels only manacle the young virgin:

> Blotched in auspicious henna
> Shrouded in shimmering crimson,
> Bound in chains of yellow gold –
> Part of his flesh, daughter of her womb.
> O great father, O great mother,
> How many blessings you gather!
> ….
>
> A diamond never cries
> A cow never speaks
> A virgin is ever voiceless.

As feminist scholars have emphasized, the mouth that produces language is viewed to bear close resemblance to the mouth constituted by woman's sexual organs, and by silencing her voice, society has silenced her desires, her expressions, her intrinsic selfhood. Pritam gives voice to the voiceless female. Speaking with her own "blistered tongue" she makes readers sensitive to the sexism festering Indian society. Simple marriage ceremonies have become extremely opulent, dowries extravagant, and gifts to the daughter and her in-laws for every rite, ritual, and festival, exorbitant. Both in India and in diasporic communities, marriages are transformed into elaborate affairs, and the quantity and quality of what is hosted for or given to the daughter reinforces the power and prestige of her father. Daughters have no rights over their natal homes; they are viewed as beautiful commodities and investments for their father's status and honor. The not-so-wealthy feel extreme pressure to squeeze out their hard-earned money to keep up with the cultural norms. While the son is desired for the accretion of his father's assets, the daughter is rejected because she represents its depletion. The economic and social demands of contemporary Indian culture are having a tragic consequence: the proportion of baby girls is declining rapidly. In India's population of 1.027 billion, the last census showed only 927 girls for every 1,000 boys – down from 945 ten years earlier. The problem is even worse in the state of Punjab: in the city of Fatehgarh Sahib, for example, the ratio of females was 750 per 1,000 males.[2] Female fetuses are being aborted to preserve the legacy, business, property, and status of fathers and their sons. Pritam's poetry helps open a window through which we can see that these gifts to/of the daughter are hideous operations of female objectification, degradation, and that they ultimately lead to female feticides. Pritam's poetry makes Heer's warning to her mother all the more urgent.

Desire definitely is the singular leitmotif of her poetic discourse. Pritam's verses overflow with a perpetual longing for love, for freedom, for an ineffable mystery, for phenomena quite distant in time and space. Perhaps these are not all that separate but intertwined at some level. In each case her yearning is framed in paradoxical and ironic twists, which provide a unique force. For instance the poem "Wish" centers on the night of Divali – the prime symbol of lights. During this popular festival celebrated across India, houses are lit with earthenware lamps (*deepa*) and the night skies dazzle with fireworks. Ironically, the refrain in this poem reads,

> *This night of Divali*
> *Is longing for lights*

In the presence of lights is their absence felt. The poet expresses her longing through the quivering lips (*farkade bulh*) of the wick, and the wavering heart of the lamp (*dive da dil chhalke*). In "A letter" we hear her passionate longing for her beloved. Taut in artistic tension,

> Night slipped
> Dreaming of you,
> I just woke up
> From my paradise.
>
> All night long, the river
> Of compassion flowed;
> Night was fulfilling those
> Promises you made.

The protagonist experienced the bliss of seven paradises. Alas it was but the nocturnal dreams that fulfilled the promises her lover had made. In this subtle dialectical play of having and losing, the absence becomes all the more acute.

Likewise, the theme of fragmentation and wholeness elusively plays out in her poem entitled "A Dream." It is about the poet's emotional ache and loneliness that manifest at night. So intense is her pain that her bones crack and break apart. But as sleep takes over, that existential despair metamorphoses into the figure of "Aum." So quickly Pritam flashes the cosmic totality on our mental screen! For Aum is not only the primal vocalic syllable of the Indian languages, it is also a configuration of the vast infinite physical universe. Discreetly though, Pritam discloses a trace of Aum – again a simultaneity of its presence and absence. Since it is scripted in the calligraphy of her fragmented limbs in her nocturnal sleep, the harmony and wholeness of Aum, sadly, is not accessible.

Yet, Pritam effectively projects the ideal, a metaphysical ideal of unity that is drawn with and by the physical contours of her body. Social, political, and religious cracks and fissures keep people from experiencing their primal unity. Cartesian dualisms of body–soul, sacred–profane, male–female, Muslim–Hindu shackle the experience of the totality of Aum. The poet longs to break through such confinements for that world of pure love and freedom.

> A love so pure was born for sure.
> But the banks of the old norms
> are just too sharp,
> Old biases and bigotries
> Are all too prickly…

Pritam's basic premise is optimistic and inspirational, for she categorically says, "*nirol ikk muhabbat tan jammi si zaroor* – a love so pure was born for sure." However, it has to be freed from the prickly old norms and oppressive conventions. The tender and diaphanous "scarf of love" (*muhabbat da daman*) has to be released from its social entanglements. In "A Morsel" she cites the case of a young woman who happened to enjoy a bit of pleasure. Soon however the news spread and the poor woman was mangled: "Her wounded hands slaughtered, her neck clawed by a single talon, her face scratched by nails." Pritam's graphic descriptions of the female victim are not for the purpose of sensationalism; rather, she identifies the perpetrators of violence – "the big-feathered, the long beaked, the crooked mouthed, the sharp nailed" so that society would stand up and confront them. The crows who forced Kanya Kumari to remain a virgin forever by deceiving Shiva, should have been brought to task and punished.

Though pain and unfulfillment permeate Pritam's poems, the driving force behind her work is the existence of pure love and Truth, and there is celebration of erotic and rapturous moments. As they filter through

Pritam's artistic intuition, rather ordinary words, gestures, and images acquire extraordinary vigor. She often repeats her verses, and their incantatory rhythms are deeply felt. In the poem "Union" our emotions stretch widely as we behold an ecstatic sky pouring out handfuls of stars (in the original Punjabi it is *"muthan bhar ke"* literally, *palm*fuls). What a contrast from the handful of rice slipping from Kanya Kumari's hands! It is the artistic genius of Pritam that in her existentially despairing lyrics she can provide bracing effects. In another intoxicating poem, the female subject enjoys the dark night bathed in rain. So blissful is her experience that the ears of the "Lofty skies above – long/To hear sounds from below/This lowly earth!" The climax of this very sensual poem:

> We do not belong to the world of gods –
> We poured out our heart's content
> We are the gift of mother earth!
> It's a night bathed in rain

Rather than direct her readers to the distant world of the gods somewhere far beyond, Pritam pulls them to this world here and now. With an erotic openness to sense experience she leads them into deeper realms of intensity.[3] From a mere twittering and meaningless subway existence "neither light nor dark" (snapshot from T.S. Eliot's *Four Quartets*), Pritam pushes us towards the nadir of pathos or the zenith of ecstasy. And with our feet planted securely on mother earth, she moves us in either direction with equal ease and spontaneity.

Some of her poems based on the folk tunes are stunning in their simplicity and melody. Their racy tunes (like Chatrik's *Kikkali Kali*) evoke the simple delights and heart-felt rhythms of Punjabi life. *Jhumar* is a folk dance patterned on a dialogue between male and female lover, and Pritam's *Jhumar* begins with

> Didn't I ask you,
> Come to the fields?
> I'll sow the seeds
> You come ploughing along …

It ends with:

My hands are colored with henna
My wrists chime with bridal bracelets
My Ranjha I am all yours:
See, I belong to nobody else…

He invites her; she invites him too. In a culture that prizes women to be silent and veiled in the confines of the home, Pritam's protagonist offers an audacious reply and a daring entry. She hearkens us back to Heer, Waris Shah's bold heroine. Tragically, Heer could not survive the stifling norms of her patriarchal society; she was murdered by the very people who brought her into life. In contrast, Pritam's heroine lives on to inspire her readers to transform their society so a Heer could live out her desires. Many of her other poems also resonate abundant joy, and recapture the natural vitality of Punjabi folk spirit coming down the generations, but each time Pritam gives them her poignant feminist twists.

The postmodern Pritam possesses a real knack for challenging society's innate assumptions. Her poetic ironies serve as lenses through which readers can begin to interrogate the inner workings of their minds. Her lyrics are effective pedagogical devices that question whether society has 20/20 vision. Do families really *honor* daughters by guarding their sexuality? By arranging marriages for them as the parents did for Heer? By giving huge dowries? By showering them with gifts all their life? By praying to Kanya Kumari that their daughters have sons? Or do they *commodify* them through their ideologies and actions? Do parents *respect* their daughters by not accepting any financial assistance or a drink of water from their married homes? Or do they *rob* them of their subjectivity? Do the codes show honor/*izzat* for women or are they codes for manliness and *his* hierarchical and patriarchal systems? Societal norms and customs criticized by our premodern poets have only gotten worse with the impact of modern technology and globalism. Subtly Pritam trains her readers to break their feudal habits and social conditioning. In her writing and in her own life she challenged conventional modes of patriarchal structure, and perhaps for that reason, the orthodox have had problems accepting her and her empowering language.

If we analyze the language of the Punjabi Pritam we discover that she is in fact speaking the "semiotic" language acclaimed by contemporary Western feminist philosophers. According to Julia Kristeva, "semiotic" is the maternal basis of language – its sounds, cadences, tones, and rhythms.[4] In her case, the semiotic bears no reference to Saussure's discipline of semiotics. Kristeva distinguishes *her* semiotic mode from the male construction and codification of language that structures univocal terms of language. For Kristeva there is a real difference between the "masculine" and the "feminine" modalities of languages. The French philosopher's distinction comes out alive in Pritam's metaphor:

> There is a truth that breeds in a bundle of vice;
> The *koel* bird may have grown up in a nest of crows,
> But she has not yet lost her primal language.
>
> ("Today...")

Starting with Sheikh Farid we heard the popular *koel* singing melodious songs perched in her beloved mango groves all over the Punjab. In the original Punjabi, Pritam describes her language as "*azlan di boli,*" which I translated as "primal language." Azal comes from the Arabic for the beginning of time, and is therefore the primordial universal language that precedes the father's linguistic divisions of Arabic, Persian, Hindi, Punjabi, or Urdu. Drenched in love, our male poets abandoned the father's syntax as well: "*jan pia dian khabran paian, mantak nahiv sabhai bhul gaian* – When I heard the news of my lover,/ I forgot all about logic and syntax" (Bullhe Shah in "All Forgotten"). Crossing genders, our poets speak the language of love that enfolds us in a kinship going back to the origins of our cosmos. The primal and polymorphous language of Pritam's *koel* is based on the singular note of Krishna's magic flute that Bullhe Shah conveyed in Chapter 2. It has the frequency that psychologically corresponds with the pre-mirror stage of Lacan, the pre-oedipal stage of Freud, and perfectly chimes in with Kristeva's maternal "semiotic." The *koel* bird intimates the poet's self-disclosure: she is Pritam who grew up in the patriarchal "nest of crows." But in spite of the Father's codes, she never lost the female language she had heard in her mother's womb. The passionate flow of the *koel*'s language is perpetual. Pritam's language is semiotic; her dynamic and spontaneous tones and rhythms are nutritious like mother's milk. With her the spiritually anguished blackness of Sheikh Farid's koel acquires yet another layer of intensity: the burning and stench absorbed in her mother's womb during the "accidents if independence" ("Helpless").

Pritam's literary flood gets her readers "incensed." They cannot merely lament or experience a poetic catharsis; they must react constructively to end the tragic plight of the oppressed. They must combat the cawing crows. The poet's psychic space is instructive and suggests possible alterations in human consciousness. Pritam departed at the age of 86, but her poetry continues to motivate her readers to action. She has mysteriously merged herself with them. Her own words testify to this uncanny reality:

> I will meet you again
> Where? How? I do not know.
> Perhaps as a spark
> Of your imagination
> I'll appear on your canvas.
>
> ("I Will Meet You Again")

For the finale of this anthology, I have chosen the opening paragraph of Pritam's "*Twarikh*" ("Date"). The poem itself is quite lengthy and delineates a gamut of devastating motions and emotions. The title marks August 15, 1947. Although the literary text denotes a specific point in time and place, Pritam maps it on the longitudes and latitudes of our vast cosmos. The seething desires voiced in its opening stanza are a relevant conclusion for this volume, *Of Sacred and Secular Desire*.

"*Twarikh*" does not begin with the day. It begins with the night heralding the dawn of independence, and its "pitch-black shawl" foreshadows the physical, emotional, and spiritual charring that ensued. India's desire for political freedom from centuries of foreign rule is going to be fulfilled. There is the desire for celebration. Intense celebration:

> Come on four species – dance
> Get up nine planets – sing
> Create an uproar in the skies that will
> Awaken our subterranean dreams…

For the momentous event the flora and fauna are invited to smile and spread their fragrance. The four species are invited to dance. Clearly, humanity is not singled out at the apex but intimately cast in a web of relations with the four categories of organisms specified in Sikh scripture – those born of egg (*andaj*), fetus (*jeraj*), sweat (*setaj*), and earth (*utbhuj*). The planets are invited to sing too. Thus the vibrant visual choreography of living beings in dance movements is synchronized with the aural symphony of the planets. They are solicited to create an uproar so loud that it would awaken the innermost desires of the people on earth. In a way the celestial scene reproduces the festive Punjabi Bhangra dance in which the audience boisterously claps and sings while it forms a circle around the dancers and the drummer. A performance at such a cosmic scale would surely arouse the slumbering psyche oblivious of its basic humanity!

Her desires succeed triumphantly in creating a wondrously complex aesthetic effect. Freedom. Exultation. An overwhelming pathos too, for inhumanity got in the way of the desired celebration. The freedom of India from years of colonial rule on August 15, 1947 came with the bloody dismemberment of the Punjab; overnight, friends turned into enemies. Ultimately then we are left with a voracious desire to fulfill that unconsummated desire. Long ago our Vedic seers proclaimed "desire" as the creative power – *iccha shakti*. With Amrita Pritam we learn to feel the power of desire, which has no limitations, no boundaries whatsoever. Her poetic canvas swirls us into a vast horizon where we must exercise our fundamental human faculties – hearing, seeing, touching, smelling, dancing, dreaming, loving. She is indeed the *koel* who speaks to us in the primal language shared by our cosmos, and we must train our ears to hear the totality of her sonic energy so that we can savor That singular note.

Amrita Pritam

ഇ രു

Chatrik

The ink in my pen is drying up,
Words from my lips are dying out;
The question raised by your death,
Can only be answered in tears.

Seasons come and seasons go,
Days are followed again by nights;
But there comes a night,
Which no day follows.

The fairy of time does not wait
Who can braid her serpentine hair?
If tears could bring good luck,
How many rivers would flow!

Carnivals broke apart and
    Wrestling bouts came to a stop,
Monsoons dried up and
    Girls' festivals closed down,
Symposiums of literati
    Are held no more;
Poets are not born any day.

Nobody used a pen like you,
Love like yours does not
    Happen everyday;
Rare is a wine lover like you –
To whom the wine pourer
    Sacrifices herself!

Your feet walked great heights,
And long is the path of this love;
With true poetry held in your hand,
You created a shrine of true art.

Countless Radhas sent you messages,
Countless more will share their secrets;
A song in your honor will strike,
Wherever people come together.

The ink in my pen is drying up

Today I Ask Waris Shah

Today I ask Waris Shah to speak from his grave,
And turn to the next page of his book of love.
You saw one Punjabi daughter weep, you wrote page after page,
Today countless daughters weep, they cry out to you Waris Shah:
Rise! O sympathizer of the afflicted! Rise! Look at your Punjab!
The land is sheeted with corpses, the Chenab is full of blood.
Somebody has poured poison into its five rivers –
And their waters are irrigating our farms and fields.
Each pore of this lush land is bursting with venom:
Redness flares up inch by inch, wrath flies high.
The poisonous breeze blows across forests –
Turning each bamboo flute into a snake.
The snakes cast a spell, and bite again and again,
The limbs of the Punjab are suddenly blue.
Songs break into silence, weaving strings snap;
Friends tear asunder, their spinning-wheels lie hushed.
Aloft with nuptial beds the rafts float away –
Branches along with swings break apart.
Lost is the flute that once played on the breath of love,
All of Ranjha's brothers forgot its art.
The blood spilt on the ground seeps into the graves,
The princesses of love weep in their sacred spots.
Today everyone is a villain, a thief of beauty and love,
From where can we bring today another Waris Shah?
Today I ask Waris Shah to speak from his grave,
And turn to the next page of his book of love.

God

You are a god in stone –
Your ice-cold touch
    Has not yet warmed;
Your emotions, asleep for ages,
    Have yet to stir.

Sacrificing their beauty
Countless women come to you,
With pulsating energy
They feel your numb limbs,
Bit by bit they stroke
Your rock hard physique,
With foreheads
    Exuding scent of flesh
They bow down to your feet.

Their warm breath
    Seething with desire,
Or the tall spiraling flames
    From the altars of fire,
Haven't melted you yet.

Their tall sinuous bodies
Lean lower and lower,
Faces fairer than the moon
Eyes darker than bees,
These countless beauties
    Embrace your statue
With every cell of their being –
Just like snakes attracted by
The scent of liquorice.

Age upon age your dry lips have devoured
Such passionate worship by your devotees!
How many beauties wilted away!
How many white arms turned to blue!
How many cups of youth have drained!
Still your parched lips continue to devour.

Like an oblation
        In your altar of fire,
I too am object,
        Smoldering
Slowly, I too will go.
This object will burn away.
A tiny part may remain:
After all I too
        Have been your worshipper...

This worshipper is making her worship –
But your platter so full of offerings
        Can barely hold me;
Like the oblation in your altar
I too am an object
        Smoldering in its fire.

How many palms have left
Their touch on your feet?
How many kisses from lips
Have congealed at your feet?
We have failed O good friend,
        We accept our defeat!
My pure virgin desires
Worship your polluted marble feet...

Gift of the Virgin

Blotched in auspicious henna
Shrouded in shimmering crimson
Bound in chains of yellow gold –
Part of his flesh, daughter of her womb.
O great father, O great mother,
How many blessings you gather!

They continue giving their charities
They continue accruing their rewards,
Bathing in the sacred Ganges...

Even now they claim,
Nothing is as great
As this great charity –
The gift of gifts –
The gift of the virgin daughter!
Give away your daughter! Get God's bounties!

A diamond never cries
A cow never speaks
A virgin is ever voiceless.

Rejoice in your charity!
Give to your heart's content,
Gift of the virgin... *kanya dan*!

Union

When you landed in my town,
The sky in ecstasy said:
Today I will pour out handfuls of stars!

When our hearts met at the landing –
Nights in white satin
Descended like rows of fairies.

When I touched your song –
My blank sheet of paper
Flooded in auspicious red.

The sun blended the henna today –
My palms are dyed deep
With both destinies.

It's a Night Bathed in Rain

It's a night bathed in rain

Having stroked the scorching sun,
It's a night bathed in rain

Pitch darkness has overtaken
The brightness of the dawn

Consciousness is nowhere to be found
A delicious sleep enfolds my flesh
The art of waking up is lost.

Lofty skies above – long
To hear sounds from below
This lowly earth!

Those intoxicated by the moon,
Why should they question
The affairs of the sun, my love

We do not belong to the world of gods
– We poured out our heart's content
We are the gift of mother earth!

It's a night bathed in rain

In Custody

My love lies in the custody of memory

Anchors have split from their banks
Oars lie severed from their boats
Waves rage in the river of my heart
Flooding down my cheeks…

Before the feet of every woman
Flows a river Chenab even today
The soles of every Sassi
Even today burn with blisters…

This life I offer you,
That life is also for you;
Those who love,
Forsake both worlds.

This heartache I solicited
My lover granted me;
In these dark clouds of pain
How do I light up a flame?

My love lies in the custody of memory

A Letter

Night slipped by
Dreaming of you,
I just woke up
From my paradise.

All night long, the river
Of compassion flowed;
Night was fulfilling those
Promises you made.

Thoughts flew
Like a flock of birds,
My lips sucked
The scent of your breath.

These walls are too high,
They block out the light;
Night stages dreams,
It shows nothing else.

In each song of mine
I write you a long letter;
How surprising, not
A line
        ever
                reaches you?

The Sound of Pain

Lips of the sky seem to quiver
Come closer, O earth, do listen to them!
These are the words of a prophet
Same as those of Jesus on the crucifix…

Who ignited the furnace of the night?
See how the sun opens its golden vessel!
O friends this is the talk of the world,
Love will be seated in the sun again…

There was talk about the deeds of the desert,
The moving caravan of life came to a halt.
Who is writing our elegy?
A star is falling from the sky…

Somebody wiped off the henna from her palms,
Then unfastened her bridal bracelet;
Who is that learned lover going away,
Leaving you to sob by the riverside?

Over there lie many graves midst trees. For the
Bier of flowers, do offer your shoulder!
The way my pen has shrouded the body of love,
Memories of its coffin will stay on…

Helpless

My mother's womb was helpless

I too am a human being – a scar
From a wound incurred
    In one of those accidents
    Of independence.
I am a mark of that event,
    Which inevitably was inscribed
    On my mother's forehead.
My mother's womb was helpless

I am that curse
Which befell humanity;
I am a product of that moment
When stars were shattering
The sun had set
And the moon too had no light.
My mother's womb was helpless

I am a scab of an old wound,
A scar on my mother's body;
I am a burden of that violence
My mother had to carry;
My mother would smell the
Stench coming from herself.

Who would know
How difficult it is
To bear flagrant violence?
For a womb to carry life?
For limbs to burn,
    For bones to char?
I am a fruit of that time
When the berries of independence
Were beginning to sprout.
My mother's womb was helpless

Light

During the night of parting,
There was a bit of light;
Or was it the wick of memory
That stirred up high?

An accident, a wound,
A scream from the heart;
At night the count of stars
Multiply over and over.

From the sky of my vision
The sun has vanished;
Its scent somehow still
Suffuses the moon.

A drop of your love
Merged with the scent;
I'll drink life's bitterness
For a sip of it.

Blasphemy

Today we sold a world,
And bought a religion;
Sheer blasphemy...

We wove a cloth of dreams,
Cut about a yard of it, and
Stitched an outfit for life...

Today from the pitcher of skies
We took off a cloudy lid, and
Sipped some moonlight!
With our songs we'll pay
For this moment that we
Mortgaged from mortality...

Happy New Year

As a tooth breaks off
From the comb of thought,
As a rip shows up
On the shirt of perception,
As a thorn pierces
The eyes full of faith,
As sleep holds
The ashes of a dream in its hands, –
That's the start of the New Year.

As a word is snuffed out
In the sentence of my heart,
As a drop of ink
Stains a letter of trust,
As a sigh escapes
From the lips of time,
As a tear lingers
On the lashes of Adam, –
That's the start of the New Year.

A blister erupts
On the tongue of love.
From the arms of culture
A bangle shatters.
From the ring of history
A gem slips out.
As the earth reads
A dark letter from the skies, –
That's the start of the New Year.

Wish

This night of Divali
Is longing for lights

Hiding and seeking, the full moon
Came over to ask in a whisper:
What color scarf did darkness
Wear tonight?

Who put an exclamation mark
On this timeless sentence?
The night of separation
Adorns my hair with a flower...

In the mortar of years,
I offered my breath as rice;
Come love, have some,
Barely a meal remains...

The lips of wick quiver,
The heart of lamp wavers;
I must call for my destiny,
As it goes fleeting by...

This night of Divali
Is longing for lights

Kanya Kumari
(Temple at the Southern Tip of the Indian Peninsula)

Waves lap into waves
Never a line between!
Like a fairy in blue
The sea sways in dance…

Nights are like pitchers
Their lips sealed tight
What misfortune! We
Cannot even have a sip…

Sacred items in her hands
Fell on the floor. A stone,
Now stands your bride.
Nothing in hand.

To you I sacrifice my being,
The world is but a stranger;
For the sake of love,
Youth became stone.

I am not the only virgin:
Earth has a million daughters;
Love turned to stone long ago,
Women are stone.

Countless lovers pursue, but
The moment of union eludes;
Fake crows still operate,
Cawing one after the other…

Crows disguise themselves,
Countless lovers end up mourning;
Logic and morality go for a price,
Counterfeit coins are struck.

Look at our life:
Grains of rice are solid stone;
Lush fruit on the branch of love
Noone has bit into…

Month of Chetar

The sun turned its back

Having gathered all its belongings
Having packed its twelfth month up

Three hundred and sixty five days
Have all been worn away

The month of *Chetar* marches in
To tie the knot of yet another year

Separation says yet again today:
To escape the six seasons of the year

"Each night belongs to me alone,
I have not shared a single one."

My lover turned his back

I gathered all my memories,
I packed my life in its bundle

g+jri release

Convention

Your love
    Trapped in convention
        Has been lost

The dust from norms
    Is thick,
I won't say much more;
The magic of its weight
    Fell on your love
Love
    Trapped in convention
        Has been lost

Love so pure must have been born.
But the banks of the old norms
    Are too sharp,
Old biases and bigotries
    Are too spiky;
The scarf of love
    Slipped by the banks
Tangled, it is caught.

Keeping a promise
    Is the color of love;
With my pledge,
    I kept it bright.
When I wanted to fly
    The bird withdrew to its nest.
Trapped in convention,
    Love is lost.

Bridges do not judge
    The color of waters,
Clear and murky
    Flowing freely by its feet.

I pity your love that
Drowned fearing
    The color of waters;
Trapped in convention,
    Love is lost.

The path of sacrifice
    Winds indeed:
Waves from the Chenab
    Take over anytime;
But is the conventional path
    Secure any more?
Before our love appraised itself,
    You took that way.
Trapped in convention,
    Love is lost.

Jhumar
Folk Dance
[A dialogue between man and woman]

Didn't I ask you,
Come to the fields?
I'll sow the seeds
You come ploughing along…

Didn't I ask you,
Come to the fields?
I'll plant the wheat, young lady,
You come watering along…

I am dropping dead from
Guarding our heaps of wheat
My bones are dissolving, and still
Thieves are lurking around.

I will demolish the house of hunger
I will lock those thieves away
I am the son of the earth,
Earth is my mother.

I will knead the fresh grain
Make warm bread with butter
My youth calls for you
Come over to me…

You are the sprouts of the mangoes
You are the blossom of time
Your youth is like the ascending moon
How can I ever measure you?

My hands are colored with henna
My wrists chime with bridal bracelets
O Ranjha I am all yours:
See, I belong to nobody else…

O Foreigner!

Sifting through the skies
East found something

A hand with a bowl of milk
With saffron mixed in it

Night cloaked in silver
Soaked in perfumes

Sky a vibrant harvest
With heaps of stars

Desires started to weave
Strands thin and delicate

Bundles burst forth of
Tender silken coils

Who gifted these?
Unfurl the four borders

Clouds are brimming
Breeze is swaying

Birds fly up
    With their wings
Branches bend down
    With their fruit

Buy me feathers
Or stay with me
O foreigner!

The Knot

The seal on my lips has broken, but
The knot in my breath is still tight...

This knot is of our spirits
This knot is of two fragrances
This knot is of our blistering sighs
This knot is of refreshing delights.

This knot is the flesh of darkness
This knot is the flesh of light;
This knot is of two supplicants
This knot is of two shrines.

If we meet let us talk
Of the sea of love
Of the ship of life
About us, the sailors...

We know their secrets -
We know their intentions –
The good sense of our earth,
The counsel given by the skies.

If we meet up let us talk,
Let us talk about lovely lips,
About sturdy feet
About tender arms...

Let us talk of dark complexions
Let us talk of healthy limbs
Shake off the dust of separation:
It belongs to back-roads.

A Morsel

Last night the life-maiden
Bit a morsel from a dream;
Don't know how this news
Reached the ears of the skies.

The big-feathered got the news,
And the long-beaked got the news,
And the crooked-mouthed got the news,
And the sharp-nailed got the news.

Her body lay naked,
Her fragrance fragmented;
She got no emotional support,
No cloth to wrap herself in.

Her morsel was snatched in a second –
Her wounded hands slaughtered
Her neck clawed by a single talon
Her face scratched by nails.

Instead of the morsel
Guilt filled her mouth;
In the skies were flying
Nights like black vultures.

Last night the life-maiden
Bit a morsel from a dream;
Don't know how this news
Reached the ears of the skies.

A Dream

Last night was painful, – as if
My bones were cracking...
Just as sleep took over
I saw my bones break apart
Then merge together
Into a silhouette of Aum.

Shawl of Radiance

This shawl of radiance
    Who can embroider it?
A niche in the skies
A flame of the sun
Who can place a lamp
    On the crest of a heart?

Had the skies been the Ganges,
It would have filled the jar;
But this river of pain,
    Who can take a sip from it?

This flame of fire that
You gave as your gift,
It burns wrapped around my heart
    Who can bear its sparks?

From our side
We ended it all
And yet a sigh
    Even now speaks of you.

This shawl of radiance
    Who can embroider it?

Recognition

When I met you,
Many lives
Pulsed in my being;
When I breathed
    A sip of your breath
Many ages throbbed
    In my forehead –

There was once a cave –
In it was a yogi and I.
And when the yogi
Took me in his arms,
Oh Allah I promise
There was a scent
That was on his lips!
Oh what *maya*! what *lila*!
Could it be you
    Who were that yogi?
Or maybe that yogi is you
Who took on your form
    And has come to me?
But I am still that one
    – And still the same scent!

I Will Meet You Again

I will meet you again
Where? How? I do not know.
Perhaps as a spark
        Of your imagination
I'll appear on your canvas
Or I may even be
That mysterious line
        On your canvas
Seeing you silently.

Or as a ray of sunshine
I may be embraced by
The colors on your palette,
Or lodged in their arms
I'll wrap your canvas
I don't know how – where
But I'll meet you for sure.

Or l may be a fountain
                                    somewhere
And like its soaring spray
I'll caress your body
With drops of water; and
Taking on a soothing shape
I'll settle on your breast...
I do not know anything else
But I do know that
Whatever time does
This life will
        keep on with me...

When the body goes,
Everything is over they say;
But the threads of memory
Are made of immutable fibers.
I'll pick those fibers
I'll spin them into thread
And I will meet you again.

The Bird of Time

The bird of time O'mother,
It neither hears nor speaks

Here are countless finials
But it won't perch anywhere

It marches on searching
    For the daily sun
Where does it dwell
Where does it come from
    Where does it go
It takes no shape or form

Rituals and oblations offer it
    Scrumptious goodies
But it will not take a peck
The bird of time O'mother
It neither hears nor speaks

O'mother I saw it with my eyes
Strolling in the forests of my mind
It was taking a bite of – that
    Moment sprouting in love

The bird of time flies on O'mother…

Today...

Your feet are pure,
    My lips are impure;
Today they will touch each other:
Either your feet will be polluted,
Or my lips will become pure
Today…

Today something will happen –
There is a truth
    That breeds in a bundle of vice;
The *koel* bird may have grown up
    In a nest of crows,
But she has not yet lost
    Her primal language of love.

The purity of your feet,
    The pollution of my lips,
Today they will cross over each other;
No, no – this cannot happen:
The touchstone remains;
    Iron turns into gold.

Hands of light will wash away
    The darkness of the storm;
Your pure feet
    My impure lips
    Today will touch…

Today something will happen…
Your pure feet
    My impure lips
Today will touch;
Your feet are pure,
    My lips will be so too today…

Date
(August 15, 1947)

This is the night of the 14th –
   My auspicious night
My lucky dawn is
   Embraced in its shawl
O pitch-black darkness!
   Take off your veil!
How many centuries I have put by
   To attain my desire today!
O woods, flowers, and trees – smile
   Spread your fragrance
Glorious spring will arrive,
   Bidding farewell to fall.
Come on four species – dance
   Get up planets – sing
Create an uproar in the skies that will
   Awaken our subterranean dreams.
O eyes glitter
   Look up above
Today my skies
   Are swelling with luster.
Suffuse us dawn with
   Your golden rays,
Extend in all four directions
   Spread our desires all over.
Blow O cool breeze
   Whirl away delights
I am India's day –
   My melodious morning is here.
O friend sing a song:
   Arouse the slumbering tunes
My courtyard rings with rapture
   My home is full of joy.
Sing a song that will
   Fill the cosmos
Sing a song dear friend
   Sing today, dear friend, sing!

CONCLUSION

In "Passage to India" written in 1871, we hear the great American poet Walt Whitman celebrate the technological marvels of his day. He begins by praising the engineers and inventors and their achievements that brought the earth closer together – the transcontinental railroad, the transoceanic cable, the Suez Canal.

> Passage to India!
> Lo, soul, seest thou not God's purpose from the first?
> The earth to be spann'd, connected by network,
> The races, neighbors, to marry and be given in marriage,
> The oceans to be cross'd, the distant brought near,
> The lands to be welded together.

Today, a century and half later, we too are celebrating the great wonders of our global interconnections – air travel, high speed internet, Skype, cell phones, global outsourcing to name just a few. Alas, in spite of such triumphant technological networks, we are unable to connect with one another at the essential human level. Insularity prevails. Geographically we may be next to each other, but racial, religious, cultural, and class divisions keep us separated. Surely, even a century and half after Whitman, "God's purpose from the first" has not been fulfilled!

The American poet regarded himself as "a true son of God," and poetry as the vehicle to bridge the world emotionally and spiritually. As we have witnessed in this anthology, our Punjabi poets were well aware of the profound influence of poetry in shaping people's worldviews, attitudes, and behavior. Centuries ago, Sheikh Farid did not write theological treatises but poetry in the local dialect that would touch the hearts of the people. Islam triumphed in winning the Indian masses precisely because of Sufi poets like Sheikh Farid. Their lyrics were sung by men and women engaged in their daily chores of ploughing the fields, spinning cotton, grinding grains, rocking their babies to sleep. Islamic ideals were thus organically infused. In the religiously and socially divided medieval Indian society, the Sikh gurus offered passionate poetry as the channel towards mutual respect and harmony. Guru Arjan collected the sublime verses of the Sikh, Muslim, Hindu poets and put into musical measures so they would resound in the psyche of the people and enable them to recognize their singular common matrix. As his predecessor had said, "Only the relisher of fragrance can recognize the flower – *rasia hovai musk ka tab phul pachanai*" (GG: 725). Recognition (*pachanai*) required a physical act as well as a cognitive realization, so the sensuousness of poetry became the way to gain insight into the oneness of humanity.

Poetry was also the vital avenue for later Punjabi Sufis who tried to unite not only Hindus and Muslims, but also Shias and Sunnis within Islam. Bullhe Shah and Waris Shah took themes and romances that were popular in the Punjab, and with their unique artistic sensibility, created mesmerizing works. Human love was their metaphor for divine love, which they expressed in language that emotionally pulled people together across borders. Now our modern and postmodern writers did express their spiritual, political, and social concerns in many different genres; however, as we have seen in the case of Bhai Vir Singh, Dhani Ram Chatrik, Firoz Din Sharaf, and Amrita Pritam, their most compelling reflections emerge in their lyrics. Even harsh reality is hard to evade when it is poetry. Much as we may want to forget Chatrik's provocative remarks "*majhab hai ikk bahana* – religion is but an excuse" or "*hai narak ikk darava te suarag hai ikk lara* – hell is only fear and heaven a false hope," it is hard to shake them out of your mind.

They are of course splendidly successful as artists, but their literary discourse is not simply art for art's sake. Whether religious or secular, medieval or postmodern, male or female, Hindu, Muslim or Sikh, our poets are invariably grounded in their socio-historic contexts. Paradoxically, their universal lyrics are a powerful response to particular situations: a calico-printer is kicked out of temples because of his biological birth, a daughter is murdered by her own parents because she wants to marry her lover from what they view is lower social status, the overt celebration of goddesses and beautiful dowry gifts covertly hide the victimization of women, the colonial rulers leave the land of the Punjab bleeding, in the name of religion the oneness of humanity is sundered apart.... The poets do not whisk us away into some world of Plato's Pure Forms; rather, they motivate us to make sense of our own twenty-first-century reality. With them we learn to navigate our lives. But importantly, they teach us without teaching. They are not missionaries. They are not preachers. They are not lecturers. Their desires overflowing from their deepest selves pour into that visceral hub where dictatorial rules and regulations never reach. Real change comes from the heart and mind – *within* each individual; not from external laws and public policies. In order to transform the world we live in, we need to change our consciousness. The material and affective textures of lyrics can do so. The harsh critic of poetry, quite well knew its force. Plato banned the poets from his Republic because "poetry feeds and waters the passions instead of drying them up."[1] Today we desperately need poetry to water our parched empathy and humanity.

Reading poetry is indeed complex, involving simultaneously the visual, perceptual, syntactic, and semantic processes. Utterly solitary, it ends up being richly communal. In the act of reading we relate with the poets directly. Eliot describes this intimate phenomenon, "my words echo thus in your mind… Disturbing the dust on a bowl of rose-leaves" (in "Burnt Norton"). Through their sensuous words we feel their touch – stirring our memories, coloring our imagination… even infuriating us, literally pushing us to action. And reading their poetry expands our social network; it bonds us with other readers. These Punjabi poets fully believed in the function of poetry as a vital communal building block. What had been known to them and practiced for centuries is theoretically elaborated by Tolstoy: if a person "becomes infected by the author's state of mind, if he feels his merging with others, then the object that calls up this state is art."[2] Only when we are infected by the desires of poets across cultures and religions will "The races, neighbors, to marry and be given in marriage…"

Whitman did not go to India. External travel was inconsequential because what mattered to the poet from New York was to enter India's literary landscape. His "Passage to India" was a courageous exploration into the primal depths of his oceanic self – a junction that is shared by humanity, a junction where the language is poetry, a junction that is infinite, a junction where the "lands are welded together." As this anthology of poetry from the other side of the globe reaches us in the West, its unique cultural metaphors and simple similes drawn from the

Punjab feed the imagination, and their acoustic speed quickens the spirit. It promotes international understanding and genuine global communication. Overall, Punjabi poetry may come to us in another diction, from another epoch, from a distant part of the world, but its "universal" desires disclose our humanity in an essential way. As Aristotle long ago said, poets speak of "incidents that might come to be," so these poets have a lot to offer as we chart our own future in our dangerously polarized world. It is reassuring that poetry and spiritual oneness are playing a major role in President Obama's visionary leadership.

NOTES

INTRODUCTION

1 Annemarie Schimmel, *The Empire of the Great Mughals: History, Art and Culture* (London: Reaktion Books, 2004), p. 118.

2 In one of the first Anglo-Sikh encounters, Charles Wilkins visited the birthplace of the Tenth Guru in Patna, and wrote an account entitled "College of the Seeks" which was published a few years later in 1788. See *Early European Accounts of the Sikhs,* edited by Ganda Singh (Calcutta, 1962), p. 75.

3 The controversy started with M.A. Macauliffe. For details see his *Sikh Religion* Vol. VI (Oxford: Clarendon University Press, 1909), p. 357.

4 For detailed study into the textual formation of the Guru Granth: Pashaura Singh, *The Guru Granth: Canon, Meaning and Authority* (Oxford, Delhi, 2000) and Gurinder Singh Mann, *The Making of Sikh Scripture* (Oxford, New York, 2001).

5 For their poetry see Nirmal Dass, *Songs of the Saints from the Adi Granth; Translation and Introduction* (Albany: State University of New York Press, 2000).

6 Kavita Daiya, *Violent Belongings: Partition, Gender, and National Culture in Postcolonial India* (Philadelphia: Temple University, 2008), pp. 7, 35.

7 Udham Singh was a young survivor of the 1919 Jallianwalla massacre, which killed close to 400 innocent civilians and left 1,200 wounded. The Indians had gathered together to celebrate the spring festival of Baisakhi in Amritsar. Udham Singh later went to the UK, and assassinated Michael O'Dywer at Caxton Hall. Though Reginald Dyer had ordered the massacre, Michael O'Dywer had been the governor of the Punjab at the time and supported Dyer.

8 Farina Mir, "Genre and Devotion in Punjabi Popular Narratives: Rethinking Cultural and Religious Syncretism" in *Comparative Studies in Society and History* 48, 3

238 OF SACRED AND SECULAR DESIRE

(July 2006) p. 730. See also her superb book, *The Social Space of Language: Vernacular Culture in British Colonial Punjab* (Berkeley: University of California Press, 2010).

[9] Ali Asani, "Sufi Poetry in the Folk Tradition of Indo-Pakistan" in *Religion & Literature*, Vol. 20, No. 1, Spring, 1988, pp. 81–94.

[10] Asani, "Sufi Poetry in the Folk Tradition of Indo-Pakistan", p. 82.

[11] Catharine Stimpson, "The Future of Memory: A Summary" in *Michigan Quarterly Review* (Winter 1987), p. 262.

[12] Annemarie Schimmel, *Mystical Dimensions of Islam* (Chapel Hill: University of North Carolina, 1975), p. 388.

[13] Christopher Shackle, "The Shifting Sands of Love" in Francesca Orsini (ed.), *Love in South Asia: A Cultural History* (Cambridge: Cambridge University Press, 2006), pp. 87–108.

[14] The change was first made by the Persian mystic Fakhuruddin Iraqi. See Annemarie Schimmel, *Mystical Dimensions of Islam*, p. 137.

[15] For more information on the Dasam Granth, see Robin Rinehart, *Debating the Dasam Granth* (AAR: Religions in Translation, 2011). For Guru Gobind Singh's Punjabi compositions on the mythic feats of Durga-Candi Punjabi poems in the Dasam Granth, see Nikky-Guninder Kaur Singh, *The Feminine Principle of the Sikh Vision of the Transcendent* (CUP, 1993) Chapter 4; and *Birth of the Khalsa: A Feminist Re-Memory of Sikh Identity* (SUNY, 2005), Chapter 2.
    The narratives on the birth and life of the first Sikh Guru did circulate in Punjabi. A good example is the B-40 Janamskahi written in 1733. It has the name of the patron, the scribe, and the artist who did some beautiful illustrations. These have been published by Surjit Hans in *B-40 Janamsakhi Guru Baba Nanak Paintings* (Amritsar: Guru Nanak Dev University, 1987).

[16] Tariq Rahman, "The Learning of Punjabi by Punjabi Muslims: a Historical Account" in *International Journal of Punjab Studies*, Vol. 8, No. 2, July–December 2001, p. 198.

[17] Hans-Georg Gadamer, *Truth and Method* (New York: Crossroad, 1989), p. 575.

[18] Gadamer, *Truth and Method*, pp. 547–8.

[19] Gadamer, *Truth and Method*, p. 548.

[20] W.B. Yeats and Shree Purohit Swami, *The Ten Principal Upanishads* (New York: Macmillan, 1937, reissued, 1975), preface, pp. 7–8.

[21] Walter Benjamin, *Illuminations: Essays and Reflections* (edited with an introduction by Hannah Arendt) (New York: Shocken Books, 1969), p. 72.

CHAPTER 1

1 S.H. Nasr, *Knowledge and the Sacred* (New York: Crossroad, 1981), p. 12.

2 For more details, see Nikky-Guninder Kaur Singh, *Sikhism: An Introduction* (London: I.B.Tauris, 2011).

3 Martin Heidegger, *Poetry Language, Thought* (Trans., Albert Hofstadter) (New York: Harper, 1971), p. 74. In Shelley's *Defence of Poetry* an identical statement is found: "...language itself is poetry...."

4 Heidegger, *Poetry, Language, Truth*, p. 72.

5 Harbans Singh, *Guru Nanak and Origins of the Sikh Faith* (Bombay: Asia Publishing House, 1969), pp. 215–6.

6 From my early work, *The Feminine Principle in the Sikh Vision of the Transcendent* (Cambridge: Cambridge University Press, 1993) to the most recent, *Sikhism: An Introduction* (London: I.B.Tauris, 2011).

7 Mary Daly, *Beyond God the Father: Toward a Philosophy of Women's Liberation* (Boston: Beacon, 1985).

8 For a fuller discussion, see Nikky-Guninder Kaur Singh, "Translating Sikh Scripture into English" in *Sikh Formations* (Routlege, UK), Vol. 3, No. 1, June 2007, pp. 1–17.

9 Philip Wheelwright, *Metaphor and Reality* (Bloomington: Indiana University Press, 1962), pp. 72–90; and Paul Ricoeur, *Interpretation Theory: Discourse and the Surplus of Meaning* (Fort Worth: Texas Christian University Press, 1976), p. 68.

10 The Sikh Gurus uniformly adopt the name of Nanak in their verse.

11 Even in an edition of *A History of the World's Religion* (New York: Macmillan, 1990), J.B. Noss entitles his chapter on Sikhism: "A study in Syncretism", pp. 234–245.

12 Carolyn Korsmeyer, *Making Sense of Taste: Food and Philosophy* (Ithaca: Cornell University Press, 2002).

13 Korsmeyer offers an accessible explanation of *rasa* in *Making Sense of Taste: Food and Philosophy*, pp. 44–5. See also Ananda Coomaraswamy, *The Hindu View of Art* (Bombay: Asia Publishing House, 1957).

14 Schimmel, *Mystical Dimensions of Islam*, p. 107.

15 Schimmel, *Mystical Dimensions of Islam*, p. 106.

16 Schimmel, *Mystical Dimensions of Islam*, p. 346.

[17] Pashaura Singh, *The Bhagats of the Guru Granth Sahib* (New Delhi: Oxford University Press, 2003), pp. 54–73.

[18] Christian Lee Novetzke, *Religion and Public Memory: A Cultural History of Saint Namdev in India* (New York: Columbia University Press, 2008). Especially, p. 1 and Chapter 6, pp. 193–216. Indira Gandhi is cited on p. 193.

[19] Popular gods and goddesses from the Hindu tradition.

[20] These include

Siddhas:	Believed to be 84 exalted persons, dwelling high in the Himalayas, after having attained immortality through the practice of yoga.
Pir:	Muslim saints.
Sur:	Gods.
Nath:	An influential yogic sect in medieval Punjab whose members practiced arduous *hatha-yoga* techniques to gain immortality.

[21] Vedas, the ancient Hindu scriptures, often appear in the Guru Granth with the "Qateb," which refers to the Semitic texts: the Torah, the Zabur, the Injil, and the Qur'an.

[22] Dharmaraja: god of judgment; Shiva: the destroyer god; Brahma: the creator god; Indra: the storm god.

[23] "raw and ripened" refers to the good and bad.

CHAPTER 2

[1] Robin Rinehart, "Interpretations of the Poetry of Bullhe Shah", *International Journal of Punjab Studies*, Vol. 3, No. 1 (New Delhi: Sage Publications, 1999), pp. 46–48; and Sant Singh Sekhon, *History of Punjabi Literature,* Vol. 2 (Patiala: Punjabi University, 1996), pp. 31–36.

[2] Sekhon, *History of Punjabi Literature*, Vol. 2, p. 92.

[3] Jeevan Deol, "Sex, Social Critique and the Female Figure in Premodern Punjabi Poetry: Varis Sahh's Hir", in *Modern Asian Studies*, Vol. 36, No. 1 (February, 2002), p. 149.

[4] Robin Rinehart, "The Portable Bullhe Shah: Biography, Categorization, and Authorship in the Study of Punjabi Sufi Poetry" in *Numen*, Vol. 46, No. 1 (1999), p. 54.

[5] Edition *Bulleh Shah dian Kafian* (Published by Mehtab Singh; Jullundur: New Book Company) No date.

[6] Robin Rinehart, "Interpretations of the Poetry of Bullhe Shah", p. 48.

[7] Jeevan Deol, "Sex, Social Critique and the Female Figure", p. 150.

8 Used by Chris Shackle for Waris Shah's text. See also, "Transition and Transformation in Varis Shah's Hir" in C. Shackle and R. Snell (eds.), *The Indian Narrative: Perspectives and Patterns* (Wiesbaden: Otto Harrosowitz, 1992), p. 262. I have used Sant Singh Sekhon's edition *Heer Waris Shah* (New Delhi: Sahitya Akademi, 2002).

9 Richard Eaton, "Sufi Folk Literature and the Expansion of Islam" in *Essays on Islam* (Oxford: Oxford University Press, 2000), pp. 189–224.

10 Ali Asani, "Sufi Poetry in the Folk Tradition of Indo-Pakistan", p. 82.

11 Robin Rinehart, "Interpretations of the Poetry of Bullhe Shah", pp. 46, 57.

12 Denis Matringe in R.S. McGregor (ed.), *Devotional Literature in South Asia: Current Research, 1985–1988* (Cambridge: Cambridge University Press, 1988), pp. 190–206.

13 S.H. Nasr, *The Heart of Islam: Enduring Values for Humanity* (New York: Harper Collins, 2004), pp. 10–11.

14 Guru Nanak's verse from Sikh scripture:
> *jab nachi tab ghughat kaisa*
> *matuki phor nirari*

(GG: 1112)

> When she dances in ecstasy,
>> How could she be veiled?
> So break the vessel and be utterly free!

15 Harjot Oberoi, *The Construction of Religious Boundaries: Culture, Identity, and Diversity in the Sikh Tradition* (Chicago: The University of Chicago Press, 1994), pp. 139–203.

16 Richard Eaton, "Court of Man, Court of God: Local Perceptions of the Shrine of Baba Farid, Pakpattan, Punjab" in *Essays on Islam* (Oxford: Oxford University Press, 2000), pp. 224–246. Also Harjot Oberoi's *The Construction of Religious Boundaries*, pp. 139–203.

17 Shackle, "Transition and Transformation in Varis Shah's Hir", p. 253.

18 Farina Mir, *The Social Space of Language: Vernacular Culture in British Colonial Punjab*, pp. 103–149.

19 The exhibition on the *Muraqqa* commissioned by the Mughal emperors Jahangir (ruled 1605–1627) and his son Shah Jahan (ruled 1627–1658) were exhibited at the Chester Beatty Library, Dublin. Summer 2010. Published by Elaine Wright, *Muraqqa': Imperial Mughal Albums from the Chester Beatty Library* (Alexandria, Va.: Art Services International, 2008).

20 Shafqat Tanveer Mirza, *Resistance themes in Punjabi literature* (Lahore: Sane-meel publications, 1992), p. 9. See also Matringe's insightful essay, "*Hir* Waris Shah" in

M. Waseem (ed.), *On Becoming an Indian Muslim: French Essays on Aspects of Syncretism* (New Delhi: Oxford University Press, 2003), pp. 208–237.

[21] Farina Mir, "Genre and Devotion in Punjabi Popular Narratives: Rethinking Cultural and Religious Syncretism", p. 754.

[22] Farina Mir, "Genre and Devotion in Punjabi Popular Narratives: Rethinking Cultural and Religious Syncretism", p. 754.

[23] Miles Irving, "The Shrine of Baba Farid at Pakpattan", cited by several scholars including Arthur Buehler in *The Sufi Heirs of the Prophet: the Indian Naqshbandiyya and the Rise of the Mediating Shaykh* (Columbia: University of South Carolina Press, 1998), p. 203.

[24] Gadamer, *Truth and Method*, p. 270.

CHAPTER 3

[1] See Farina Mir's very informative chapter, "Forging a Language Policy" in *The Social Space of Language*, pp. 27–61.

[2] Bernard S. Cohn, *Colonialism and its Forms of Knowledge: the British in India* (Princeton: Princeton University Press, 1996), pp. 21–22.

[3] R. J. Moore, "The Composition of 'Wood's Education Despatch'" in *The English Historical Review*, Vol. 80, No. 314 (January, 1965), pp. 70–85.

[4] Arvind Mandair, *The Specter of the West: Sikhism, India, Postcoloniality, and the Politics of Translation* (New York: Columbia University Press, 2010), pp. 204–239.

[5] Chris Shackle has a useful chapter, "Some Observations on the Evolution of Modern Standard Punjabi" in *Sikh History and Religion in the Twentieth Century*. Edited by J.T. O'Connell, M. Israel, W.G. Oxtoby (University of Toronto, Centre for South Asian Studies, 1988), pp. 101–109.

[6] Quoted by Rahman, "Learning of Punjabi by Punjabi Muslims", p. 195.

[7] Both cited by Tim Allender, *Ruling Through Education: The Politics of Schooling in Colonial Punjab* (Elgin, IL; Berkshire, UK; and New Delhi: New Dawn Press, 2006). Montgomery is cited on p. 93; Lawrence, p. 94.

[8] Sir Charles James Napier (edited by W.F.P. Napier), *Defects, Civil and Military, of the Indian Government* (London: Charles Westerton, 1853), p. 365.

[9] Christopher Shackle, "Some Observations on the Evolution of Modern Standard Punjabi", p. 103.

[10] Paul Brass, *Language, Religion and Politics in North India* (Cambridge: Cambridge University Press, 1974), p. 288.

11 For more details see Nikky-Guninder Kaur Singh, *Cosmic Symphony: The Early and Later Poems of Bhai Vir Singh* (New Delhi: Sahitya Akademi, 2008).

12 I have developed it more fully in my introduction to *Cosmic Symphony*.

13 Ellison Banks Findly, *Nur Jahan: Empress of India* (New York: Oxford University Press, 1993).

14 F. S. Aijazuddin, *Sikh Portraits by European Artists* (London, NY: Sotheby Parke Bernet, 1979), p. 30.

15 Richard Wolf, "The Poetics of 'Sufi' practice: Drumming, Dancing, and complex agency at Madho Lal Husain (and beyond)" in *American Ethnologist*, Vol. 3, No. 2, p. 253.

16 In the introduction to Feroz Din Sharaf, *Nuri Darshan* (anthology on Sikh themes) (Ludhiana: Lahore Book Shop, no date), p. 12. Dr. Mohan Singh's introduction is dated 24.2.34.

17 Atamjit Singh, "The Language Divide in Punjab" for the Academy of the Punjab in North America, *South Asian Graduate Research Journal*, Vol. 4, No. 1, Spring 1997, footnote 60.

18 According to Dr. Mohan Singh, Sharaf was born in Lahore (*Nuri Darshan*, p. 5). According to Darshan Singh Awara, editor of Sharaf's poety in two volumes, *Sharaf Racnavali* (Patiala: Department of Languages, 1973), the poet was born in village Tola Nangal in the Raja Sansi district of Amritsar (*Sharaf Racnavali*, Vol. 1), pp. 9–10.

19 Ahmad Ghabin, *Hisba, Arts and Craft in Islam* (Wiesbaden: Otto Harrassowitz, 2009), pp. 232–234.

20 *The Collected Works of Mahatma Gandhi*, Vol. 19 (Delhi: The Publications Division, Ministry of Information and Broadcasting. Government of India, 1967), p. 399.

21 *Sharaf Racnavali* Vol. 1. Darshan Singh Awara (ed.) (Patiala: Department of Languages, 1973), p. 15.

22 Popularly known as the five k-s, they are worn as symbols of Sikh identity: *kesh* (unshorn hair), *kangha* (comb), *kara* (bracelet), *kacha* (underpants), and *kirpan* (sword).

23 Pritam Singh, "The idea of Punjabiyat," *Himal Southasian*, Vol. 23, No. 5, May 2010, pp. 55–57.

CHAPTER 4

[1] Urvasi Butalia, *The Other Side of Silence: Voices from the Partition of India* (New Delhi: Viking, 1998).

[2] Nikky-Guninder Kaur Singh, "Female Feticide in the Punjab" in *Imagining the Fetus* (American Academy of Religion: Oxford University Press, 2009), pp. 120–136. Also, "The Kanjak and the Broken Bangles" in *South Asian Review* (University of Pittsburgh, 29/2 (2008), pp. 109–32.

[3] In Pritam's poetry, literary scholars tend to focus on the theme of "sublime nationalism" rather than the sensuous. See for example Akshaya Kumar, *Poetry, Politcs and Cutlure: Essays on Indian Texts and Contexts* (New Delhi: Routledge, 2009), pp. 321–323.

[4] Julia Kristeva, *In the Beginning was Love: Psychoanalysis and Faith* (Trans., Arthur Goldhammer) (New York: Columbia University Press, 1987).

CONCLUSION

[1] Republic, Book X, 606.

[2] Leo Tolstoy, *What is Art?* Translated by Richard Pevear and Larissa Volokhonsky (London: Penguin Classics, 1995), p. 121.

BIBLIOGRAPHY

PRIMARY SOURCES

Bhai Vir Singh Rachnavali, Vol. I (Collection of Poetry) (Patiala: Department of Languages, 1972).

Bullhe Shah dian Kafian. Published by Mehtab Singh (Jullundur: New Book Company; no date).

Chatrik, Dhani Ram, *Sufi Khana* (Amritsar: Punjabi Sahitak Prakashan, 2001).

Heer Waris Shah. Edited by Sant Singh Sekhon (New Delhi: Sahitya Akademi, 2002).

Kalam Bullhe Shah. Edited by Dr. Gurdev Singh (Ludhiana: Lahore Book Shop, 2002).

Pritam, Amrita, *Kagaz Te Canvas Ton Pehlan* (Delhi: Shilalekh, 2004).

———, *Main Tainun Phir Milangi* (Delhi: Shilalekh, 2004).

Sabdarath: Sri Guru Granth Sahibji, Vol. 1–4 (Amritsar: Shiromani Gurdwara Prabandhak Committee, 1969).

Sharaf Racnavali Vol. 1 and 2. Darshan Singh Awara (ed.), (Patiala: Department of Languages, 1972/1973).

SECONDARY SOURCES

Aijazuddin, F. S., *Sikh Portraits by European Artists* (London and New York: Sotheby Parke Bernet, 1979).

Allender, Tim, *Ruling Through Education: The Politics of Schooling in Colonial Punjab* (Elgin, IL; Berkshire, UK; and New Delhi: New Dawn Press, 2006).

Asani, Ali, "Sufi Poetry in the Folk Tradition of Indo-Pakistan" in *Religion & Literature*, Vol. 20, No. 1 (Spring 1988), pp. 81–94.

———, *Celebrating Muhammad: Images of the Prophet in Popular Muslim Poetry* (Columbia: University of South Carolina Press, 1995).

Benjamin, Walter, *Illuminations: Essays and Reflections* (with an introduction by Hannah Arendt) (New York: Shocken Books, 1969).

Bose, Sugata and Ayesha Jalal, *Modern South Asia: History, Culture, Political Economy* (New York: Routledge, 1998).

Brass, Paul, *Language, Religion and Politics in North India* (Cambridge, MA: Cambridge University Press, 1974).

Buehler, Arthur, *The Sufi Heirs of the Prophet: the Indian Naqshbandiyya and the Rise of the Mediating Shaykh* (Columbia: University of South Carolina press, 1998).

Butalia, Urvasi, *The Other Side of Silence: Voices from the Partition of India* (New Delhi: Viking, 1998).

Callewaert, Winand M. and Peter G. Friedlander, *The Life and Works of Raidas* (New Delhi: Manohar, 1992).

Chahil, Pritam Singh (Trans.), *Sri Guru Granth Sahib*, 4 vols. (New Delhi: the translator, 1992).

Chandan, Amarjit, *Sonata for Four Hands* (UK: Arc Publications, 2010).

Cohn, Bernard, *Colonialism and its Forms of Knowledge: The British in India* (Princeton: Princeton University Press, 1996).

Coomaraswamy, Ananda, *The Hindu View of Art* (Bombay: Asia Publishing House, 1957).

Daiya, Kavita, *Violent Belongings: Partition, Gender, and National Culture in Postcolonial India* (Philadelphia: Temple University, 2008).

Dalmia, Vasudha (introduction to and compilation of) *Myths, Saints, and Legends in Medieval India* by Charlotte Vaudeville (New York: Oxford University Press, 1996).

Daly, Mary, *Beyond God the Father: Toward a Philosophy of Women's Liberation* (Boston: Beacon Press, 1985).

Dass, Nirmal, *Songs of the Saints from the Adi Granth; Translation and Introduction* (Albany: State University of New York Press, 2000).

Deol, Jeevan, "Sex, Social Critique and the Female Figure in Premodern Punjabi Poetry: Varis Shah's Hir", *Modern Asian Studies*, Vol. 36, No. 1 (February, 2002), pp. 141–71.

Eaton, Richard, "Sufi Folk Literature and the Expansion of Islam" and "Court of Man, Court of God: Local Perceptions of the Shrine of

Baba Farid, Pakpattan, Punjab" in *Essays on Islam* (Oxford: Oxford University Press, 2000).

Findly, Ellison Banks, *Nur Jahan: Empress of India* (New York: Oxford University Press, 1993).

Gadamer, Hans-Georg, *Truth and Method* (New York: Crossroad, 1989).

The Collected Works of Mahatma Gandhi, Vol. 19 (Delhi: The Publications Division, Ministry of Information and Broadcasting, Government of India, 1967).

Ghabin, Ahmad, *Hisba, Arts and Craft in Islam* (Wiesbaden: Otto Harrassowitz, 2009).

Gilmartin, David and Bruce B. Lawrence (eds.), *Beyond Turk and Hindu: Rethinking Religious Identities in Islamicate South Asia* (Gainesville: University of Florida Press, 2000).

Gilmartin, David, "Partition, Paksitan, and South Asian History: In Search of a Narrative" *The Journal of Asian Studies*, Vol. 57, No. 4 (November, 1998), pp. 1068–1095.

Gold, Daniel, *The Lord as Guru: Hindi Sants in North Indian Tradition* (New York: Oxford University Press, 1987).

Grierson, George, *The Modern Vernacular Literature of Hindustan* (Calcutta: Asiatic Society, 1889).

Hawley, J.S. and Mark Juergensmeyer, *Songs of the Saints of India* (New York: Oxford University Press, 1988).

Heidegger, Martin, *Poetry Language, Thought* (Trans., Albert Hofstadter) (New York: Harper & Row, 1971).

Khan, Yasmin, *The Great Partition: The Making of India and Pakistan* (New Haven: Yale University Press, 2007).

Kohli, S.S., *History of Punjabi Literature* (Delhi: National Book Shop, 1993).

Korsmeyer, Carolyn, *Making Sense of Taste: Food and Philosophy* (Ithaca: Cornell University Press, 2002).

Krishna, Lajwanti Rama, *Punjabi Sufi Poets, A.D. 1460–1900* (New Delhi: Ashajanak Publications, 1973)

Kristeva, Julia, *In the Beginning was Love: Psychoanalysis and Faith* (Trans., Arthur Goldhammer) (New York: Columbia University Press, 1987).

Kumar, Akshaya, *Poetry, Politics and Culture: Essays on Indian Texts and Contexts* (New Delhi: Routledge, 2009).

Latif, Syad Muhammad, *History of the Punjab* (New Delhi: Kalyani Publishers, 1994).

Lopes, Donald (ed.), *The Religions of India in Practice* (Princeton: Princeton University Press, 1995).

Lorenzen, David (ed.), *Bhakti Religion in North India: Community Identity and Political Action* (New York: State University of New York Press, 1995).

———, *Praises to a Formless God: Nirguni Texts from North India* (New York: State University of New York Press, 1996).

Macauliffe, M.A., *Sikh Religion* Vol. VI (Oxford: Clarendon University Press, 1909).

Madra, Amandeep Singh and Paramjit Singh, *Warrior Saints: Three Centuries of the Sikh Military Tradition* (London: I.B.Tauris, in association with the Sikh Foundation, 1999).

Maken, G.S. *The Essence of Sri Guru Granth Sahib*, 5 vols. (Chandigarh: Guru Tegh Bahadur Educational Centre, 2001).

Mandair, Arvind, *The Specter of the West: India, Postcoloniality, and the Politics of Translation* (New York: Columbia University Press, 2010).

Mandair, Arvind and C. Shackle (eds. and trans.), *Teachings of the Sikh Gurus: Selections from the Sikh Scriptures* (London, New York: Routledge, 2005).

Mann, Gurinder Singh, *The Goindval Pothis: The Earliest Extant Source of the Sikh Canon* (Harvard Oriental Series, Vol. 51; Cambridge: Cambridge University Press, 1997).

———, *The Making of Sikh Scripture* (New York: Oxford University Press: 2001).

Matringe, Denis in McGregor, R.S. (ed.), *Devotional Literature in South Asia: Current Research, 1985–1988* (Cambridge: Cambridge University Press, 1988).

———, *"Hir* Waris Shah*"* in M. Waseem (ed.), *On Becoming an Indian Muslim: French Essays on Aspects of Syncretism* (New Delhi: Oxford University Press, 2003), pp. 208–237.

Mcleod, W.H., *Textual Sources for the Study of Sikhism* (Chicago: University of Chicago Press, 1990).

Metcalf, Barbara (ed.), *Islam in South Asia in Practice* (Princeton: Princeton University Press, 2009).

Miller, Barbara Stoler, *Love Song of the Dark Lord: Jayadeva's Gitagovinda* (New York: Columbia University Press, 1977).

Mir, Farina, "Genre and Devotion in Punjabi Popular Narratives: Rethinking Cultural and Religious Syncretism" in *Comparative Studies in Society and History* Vol. 48, No. 3 (July, 2006), pp. 727–58.

———, *The Social Space of Language: Vernacular Culture in British Colonial Punjab* (Berkeley: University of California Press, 2010).

Mirza, Shafqat Tanveer, *Resistance themes in Punjabi literature* (Lahore: Sang-e-Meel Publications, 1992).

Mitchell, Lisa, *Language, Emotion, and Politics in South India: The Making of a Mother Tongue* (Bloomington: University of Indiana Press, 2009).

Moore, R. J., "The Composition of 'Wood's Education Despatch'" in *The English Historical Review*, Vol. 80, No. 314 (January, 1965), pp. 70–85.

Napier, Sir Charles James (ed.), *Defects, Civil and Military, of the Indian Government* by W.F.P. Napier (London: Charles Westerton, 1853).

Nasr, S.H., *The Heart of Islam: Enduring Values for Humanity* (San Francisco: HarperCollins, 2004).

———, *Knowledge and the Sacred* (New York: Crossroad, 1981).

Nijhawan, Michael, *Dhadi Darbar: Religion, Violence, and the Performance of Sikh History* (New Delhi: Oxford University Press, 2006).

Noss, J.B., *A History of the World's Religion* (New York: Macmillan, 1990).

Novetzke, Christian Lee, *Religion and Public Memory: A Cultural History of Saint Namdev in India* (New York: Columbia University Press, 2008).

Oberoi, Harjot, *The Construction of Religious Boundaries: Culture, Identity, and Diversity in the Sikh Tradition* (Chicago: University of Chicago Press, 1994).

Orsini, Francesca (ed.), *Love in South Asia: A Cultural History* (Cambridge: Cambridge University Press, 2006).

———, *The Hindi Public Sphere 1920–1940: Language and Literature in the Age of Nationalism* (New York: Oxford University Press, 2002).

Pollock, Sheldon (ed.), *Literary Cultures in History: Reconstructions from South Asia* (Berkeley: University of California Press, 2003).

Rahman, Tariq, "The Learning of Punjabi by Punjabi Muslims: a Historical Account" in the *International Journal of Punjab Studies*, Vol. 8, No. 2 (July–December, 2001), pp. 187-224.

Ricoeur, Paul, *Interpretation Theory: Discourse and the Surplus of Meaning* (Fort Worth: Texas Christian University Press, 1976).

Rinehart, Robin, "Interpretations of the Poetry of Bullhe Shah" *International Journal of Punjab Studies*, Vol. 3, No. 1 (New Delhi: Sage Publications, 1996), pp. 45–63.

———, "The Portable Bullhe Shah: Biography, Categorization, and Authorship in the Study of Punjabi Sufi Poetry" in *Numen*, Vol. 46, No. 1. (1999), pp. 43–87.

———, *Debating the Dasam Granth* (Oxford: Oxford University Press, 2011).

Sasson, Vanessa, *Imagining the Fetus: The Unborn in Myth, Religion and Culture* (Oxford, New York: Oxford University Press, 2008).

Schimmel, Annemarie, *Islamic Literatures of India* (Wiesbaden: Otto Harrassowitz, 1973).

———, *Mystical Dimensions of Islam* (Chapel Hill: University of North Carolina Press, 1975).

———, *The Empire of the Great Mughals: History, Art and Culture* (London: Reaktion Books 2004).

Schomer, Karen and W.H. McLeod (eds.), *The Sants: Studies in a Devotional Tradition of India* (Delhi: Motilal Banarsidass, 1987).

Sekhon, Sant Singh and K.S. Duggal, *A History of Punjabi Literature* (New Delhi: Sahitya Akademi, 1992).

Sekhon, Sant Singh, *History of Punjabi Literature*, 2 vols. (Patiala: Punjabi University, 1996).

———, (Translator) *The Love of Hir and Ranjha* (Ludhiana: Punjab Agricultural University, 1978).

Serebryakov, I., *Punjabi Literature: A Brief Outline* (Moscow: Nauka Publishing House, Central Department of Oriental Literature, 1968).

Shackle, Christopher, *An Introduction to the Sacred Language of the Sikhs,* (London: SOAS, University of London, 1983).

———, "Some Observations on the Evolution of Modern Standard Punjabi" in *Sikh History and Religion in the Twentieth Century* by J. T. O'Connell, M. Israel, W.G. Oxtoby (eds.) (University of Toronto: Centre for South Asian Studies, 1988).

———, "Transition and Transformation in Varis Shah's Hir" in C. Shackle and R. Snell (eds.) *The Indian Narrative: Perspectives and Patterns* (Wiesbaden: Otto Harrosowitz, 1992).

———, "The Shifting Sands of Love" in Francesca Orsini (ed.), *Love in South Asia: A Cultural History* (Cambridge: Cambridge University Press, 2006).

Singh, Amritjit and Judy Ray (Trans.), *The Circle of Illusion: Poems by Gurcharan Rampuri* (San Francisco: Weavers Press, 2011).

Singh, Atamjit, "The Language Divide in Punjab", *Academy of the Punjab in North America, South Asian Graduate Research Journal,* Vol. 4, No. 1, (Spring 1997).

Singh, Attar (ed.), *Socio-Cultural Impact of Islam on India* (Chandigarh: Punjab University, 1976).

Singh, Ganda (ed.), *Early European Accounts of the Sikhs* (Calcutta, 1962).

Singh, Gopal, *Sri Guru Granth Sahib: English Version* (Chandigarh: The World Sikh University Press, 1978).

Singh, Harbans, *Aspects of Punjabi Literature* (Ferozpur: Bawa Publishing House, 1961).

———, *Guru Nanak and Origins of the Sikh Faith* (Bombay: Asia Publishing House, 1969).

———, *Bhai Vir Singh* (Makers of Indian Literature) (New Delhi: Sahitya Akademy, 1972).

Singh, Manmohan. Trans. *Sri Guru Granth Sahib*, 8 vols. (Amristsar: SGPC, 1969).

Singh, Nikky-Guninder Kaur, *Feminine Principle of the Sikh Vision of the Transcendent* (Cambridge: Cambridge University Press, 1993).

———, *The Name of My Beloved: Verses of the Sikh Gurus* (New Delhi: Penguin, 2001).

———, *Birth of the Khalsa: A Feminist Re-Memory of Sikh Identity* (New York: State University of New York Press, 2005).

———, "Translating Sikh Scripture into English" in *Sikh Formations* (Routledge, UK), Vol. 3, No. 1 (June 2007), pp. 1–17.

———, "The Kanjak and the Broken Bangles" in *South Asian Review* (University of Pittsburgh, Vol. 29, No. 2 (2008), pp. 109-32.

———, *Cosmic Symphony: The Early and Later Poems of Bhai Vir Singh* (New Delhi: Sahitya Akademi, 2008).

———, *Sikhism: An Introduction* (London: I.B.Tauris, 2011).

Singh, Pashaura, *The Guru Granth: Canon, Meaning and Authority* (New Delhi: Oxford University Press, 2000).

———, *The Bhagats of the Guru Granth Sahib* (New Delhi: Oxford University Press, 2003).

Singh, Pritam, "The idea of Punjabiyat," *Himal Southasian*, Vol. 23, No. 5 (May 2010), pp 55–57.

Stimpson, Catherine, "The Future of Memory: A Summary" in *Michigan Quarterly Review*, Vol. 26, No. 1 (Winter 1987), pp. 259-265.

Suvorova, Anna, *Muslim Saints of South Asia: The Eleventh to Fifteenth Centuries* (New York: RoutledgeCurzon, 2004).

Syed, Najm Hossain, *Recurrent Patterns in Punjabi Poetry* (Lahore: Punjab Adbi Markaz, 1978).

Talib, G.S. (Trans.), *Sri Guru Granth Sahib*, 4 vols. (Patiala: Punjabi University, 1984).

Tandon, Prakash, *Punjabi Century, 1857-1947* (Berkeley: University of California Press, 1961).

Tolstoy, Leo, *What is Art?* (Trans., Richard Pevear and Larissa Volokhonsky) (London: Penguin Classics, 1995).

Uberoi, Mohan Singh, *A History of Punjabi Literature*, 1100–1932 (Jalandhar: Bharat Prakashan, 1971).

Vaudevile, Charlotte, *Myths, Saints, and Legends in Medieval India* (compiled and with an introduction by Vasudha Dalmia) (New York: Oxford University Press, 1996).

Waseem, M. (ed.), *On Becoming an Indian Muslim: French Essays on Aspects of Syncretism* (New Delhi: Oxford University Press, 2003).

Wheelwright, Philip, *Metaphor and Reality* (Bloomington: Indiana University Press, 1962).

Wolf, Richard, "The Poetics of 'Sufi' practice: Drumming, Dancing, and Complex Agency at Madho Lal Husain (and beyond)" in *American Ethnologist*, Vol. 3, No. 2, pp. 246–268.

Zelliot, Eleanor and Rohini Mokashi-Punekar (eds.), *Untouchable Sants: An Indian Phenomenon* (New Delhi: Manohar, 2005).